One chil
teaches us
in God's family

Jacob's
Journey

JEANIE SHAW

DPI
DISCIPLESHIP
PUBLICATIONS
INTERNATIONAL

Jacob's Journey

Printed in the United States of America

ISBN 1-57782-161-0

Cover & Interior Design: Tony Bonazzi
Front Cover Photo–Jacob Shaw and Jordan: Jeanie Shaw and Laura Meyer
Back Cover Photo–Shaw/Miller Family: Laura Meyer

To Jacob, whose introduction into my life and heart has brought me such great joy and a deeper and richer understanding of God's love.

And to the rest of the family—Wyndham, the love of my life, and Melissa, Kevin, Kristen and Sam—your love for God, for me, for Jacob, for one another and those around you inspires me, convicts me, makes me deeply thankful and very, very happy.

I love you all.

The Shaw family in Romania before Jacob's adoption

Jacob at the orphanage before his adoption

Contents

FOREWORD

As I write this foreword for *Jacob's Journey*, four deep personal emotions rise within me. The first is my ever-deepening admiration, respect and heartfelt love for my wife Jeanie. She had the heart not only to write this book but to inspire, persuade and convict our entire family to begin Jacob's journey, the real experience of our family's adoption of our fourth child. She is a Proverbs 31 woman in every way, more precious than jewels, clothed with strength and dignity, laughing at the days to come and holding out her hands to the poor—especially the orphans of Romania. This book and all it conveys merely reveal a corner of her heart, which is so filled with love she often makes me feel anemic in that quality by comparison. Honey, I want to thank you and praise you from the heart of a husband who not only trusts in your love for him but has learned much from your love for Jacob and so many more.

The second emotion is how much love I have grown to have for Jacob, a boy not born to me biologically, but attached now to my heart as tightly as those children who were. His circumstances at first grabbed my sympathy and compassion, but his zest for life, magnetic smile, responsive heart and effort to change have moved me from compassion and unconditional love to tightly bonded affection and friendship as father and son. He has tested my patience, challenged my physical strength far sooner than I imagined and taught me many "survival tactics" learned from twelve years of making the most of nothing. I am glad he is on my side and look forward to continuing our "journey" toward manhood and best friendship together. Jake, I only wish we could have started our journey together sooner than we did, but I promise to make the most of what God has given us.

The third emotion is that of my love for Melissa, Kristen and Sam—my other three children and older sisters and brother to Jacob. They have amazed me by their unselfish embracing of

our decision to adopt and of Jacob himself. We of course
included them in the process, and they did not get on board
without honest personal struggle. They continue the journey
with many more honest personal struggles. But they have never
wavered in sharing the load and filling their spot on the team
of building our family into a haven and joy for not only Jacob,
but for us all. My family is my greatest joy beyond my salvation. I don't tell them enough how proud I am of each one indi-
vidually and all of them collectively. I write this with tears in my
eyes, high above the Atlantic, headed for a home-cooked meal
with most of them. I hope this statement of praise will outlast
me as a tribute to each of them for the way they have made this
husband and father the most blessed man on earth.

Melissa, you have been an incredible big sister and oldest
child to each of your siblings and to your mom and me. Your
reliable character, your pursuit of excellence, your expressions
of love for God and each of us, and your laugh attacks have
made you a great role model and glue for us all. Kris, you have
been the emotional center of our family in many ways, keep-
ing us in touch with each other's feelings, fears and faith both
when they were pretty and when they were ugly. You have
soaked Jacob in hugs and kisses and reminded all of us that
we need to be soaked in love continually. You are an incredible example of an overcomer, and have inspired us all to be
the same. Sam, you are a man after my own heart—truly the
gift of a much desired first son. I could not have asked for a
better male companion from birth to adulthood. Of all the
kids, you have borne the greatest tests of selflessness in terms
of time given and given up for Jacob because of your birth
order and common gender. Even when you have struggled,
it has been honest, open and always ending with a recommit-
ment to love and serve as a model older brother. Jacob loves
and respects you and will only fully appreciate the role model
you have been in years to come. Writing this makes me
feel more keenly the reality of your leaving home in a few
months. The greatest comfort is in knowing you are ready for

your journey in even greater ways because of Jacob's journey, and we will continue to be best friends as you travel God's path for your life.

Finally the fourth emotion is my utmost gratitude to God for his grace in giving me the desire of my heart in a family sent from heaven. We all have been taught by God how to love, forgive, persevere and overcome our sin, selfishness and differences. We are not perfect by any means, but we have reaped the benefit of following God's perfect plan for imperfect people in loving each other deeply and from the heart. The Psalmist expresses my heart along with his own when he says,

> Sons are a heritage from the Lord,
>   children a reward from him.
> Like arrows in the hands of a warrior
>   are sons born in one's youth.
> Blessed is the man
>   whose quiver is full of them.
> They will not be put to shame
>   when they contend with their enemies in the gate.
>   (Psalm 127:3-5)

God has made that promise real in the Shaw family and motivated me to want to share the good news of godly families with parents, teenagers, preteens, toddlers and infants...as well as orphans and abandoned children of all types.

Jacob's journey into our family has convinced me more than ever of the need for godly champions to rise up for the millions of lonely children who have no families or are trapped in families that do not know how to share God's love. More families need to learn how to love each other as God designed fathers and mothers, parents and children, and brothers and sisters to live together in a corner of heaven here on earth.

I commend to you *Jacob's Journey*. May you be encouraged and inspired by our family's journey and by the efforts of my wife to share it with you.

Wyndham Shaw
June 2001

Acknowledgments

So many individuals have been there to help Jacob on his journey. I am forever grateful. Thanks to each of you who have touched his life and therefore have touched mine as well.

Thanks to my husband and children for your faithful love, tireless support and encouragement in the writing of this book.

To my parents and sisters, I am grateful for your love. A special thanks to my sister Carolyn Harrell for your first edits and writing support. You make me feel very believed in.

I also want to express appreciation to my sister-in-law Mary Ann Bisher for the way you love Jacob and make him feel so special; to Pat Gempel who first put a child in Wyndham's arms at Orphanage #4. (It worked.) Thank you for your practice of true religion and changing our lives. And Bob, your steady wisdom is so needed. Roxanne, you were with me the first time I met Jacob and made our party so special. Randy and Kay, you have been so instrumental in our lives and so encouraging with Jacob. Gordon and Theresa, you are such dear friends and make our kids your kids.

To the Pierce family, for taking Jacob into your home like your fourth son; and to the Malutinoks and Fallers who have given so much as well, as have Jimmy and Maria Rogers.

To the Jenkins, you are dear friends and have loved watching Jacob "the fish," as you warmly call him, swim in your pool. I thank the Astones and Devlins for this as well. Thank you Phil Arsenault for your love and commitment to Jacob and for teaching him the drums.

Ileana Grosu, without your determination we never would have been able to adopt Jacob. Thank you for bearing with me. And to Los Ninos, thank you for all your help and patience as I went about this in an unorthodox way, having spent so much time in Romania. Maria, I am forever grateful for the love you showed Jacob and his friends when none but God was watching. Radu, thank you for going the extra mile trekking the bumpy roads in your Trobby to see Jacob and reassure him. Also to Aileen, I thank you for your attention to the kids at #4 in Bucharest. For the entire Bucharest Church of Christ I am grateful for your being family to Jacob and to us. Brian and Caryn, thanks for your care in planting the church and having such a heart for the children. Matt Genese, thank you for being a great friend to Jacob in Romania and when he first arrived in America. Thank you to Kent Brand who helped me understand things Jacob was going through and to HOPE for Children for all you do on behalf of abandoned children. Julia Hannon, you have put skin on my dream for children in Massachusetts, and I am amazed at all you have been able to accomplish. To all the foster and adoptive families, your camaraderie is so valuable and you are all heroes. Thank you Ilona Sewell for the tutoring and educational direction that helped so much.

Every so often you find teachers and instructors who go the extra mile to help. Thank you Tom Ciarlone, Betty Cook, Noreen Abati for being there when Jacob needed you and still needs you. I appreciate the instructors and coaches who have believed in Jacob like Bill Rowe, the soccer coach, and Steve Nugent, who helped Jacob with confidence in karate lessons, the camp counselors and all the teachers in Kingdom Kids preteen classes. I am so grateful to the Boston Church of Christ for the endless support to our children, and your commitment to the "adoption fund," enabling many more to adopt.

A special thanks to the Kohas, Bathons and Cattos for contributing so much to keep the work for the kids in Romania going and growing. To the Tromblys and Boltons, thank you. Jim and Sarah, what you are doing for the children is heroic. Thank you wonderful children of the HOPE *worldwide* Family Center. You love Jacob and love us and your love is so valuable. Thank you to the Rushtons; you have been with us in this. And Laura Meyer, you have been so fun for Jacob.

Sheila Jones, you have been incredible in helping this sound right, and your encouragement has meant a lot. To Vickie Boone and all the DPI staff, you guys are amazing.

ANYWAY

People are unreasonable, illogical and self-centered,
LOVE THEM ANYWAY.

If you do good, people will accuse you of selfish, ulterior motives,
DO GOOD ANYWAY.

If you are successful,
you win false friends and true enemies,
SUCCEED ANYWAY.

The good you do will be forgotten tomorrow,
DO GOOD ANYWAY.

Honesty and frankness make you vulnerable,
BE HONEST AND FRANK ANYWAY.

What you spent years building may be destroyed overnight,
BUILD ANYWAY.

People really need help
but may attack you if you help them,
HELP PEOPLE ANYWAY.

Give the world the best you have
and you'll get kicked in the teeth,
GIVE THE WORLD THE BEST YOU'VE GOT ANYWAY.

You see, in the final analysis,
it is between you and God.
IT NEVER WAS BETWEEN YOU AND THEM ANYWAY.

(Found on the wall of Shishu Bhavan, a children's home in Calcutta)

INTRODUCTION

Come Journey with Me

Several thousand miles have been covered since early this morning. We have not yet reached our final destination, but the journey has begun.

Jacob, eleven, our newly adopted son is at my side. He has no idea how much his coming into our lives has taught me about our amazing God. Never has our Father's love been more vivid, his power more awe-inspiring, and his orchestration more wondrous.

The preceding two paragraphs were written in August of 1998. I have now compiled our story and the insights I have gained about God's adoption of all of us into his family. My hope is that the sharing of this story will move your heart, as it has mine, to see the breadth, depth, length and height of God's love in his quest to adopt each of us.

In each chapter I will tell a story of an experience we had in adopting Jacob into our family. Then the "footprints" will walk the story into your heart as you compare your adoption into God's family. Beginning and ending Scripture selections will reinforce the spiritual insight gained in each chapter. In the back of the book you will find application questions and additional scriptures for the individual chapters to help you further grasp the point at hand.

Come journey with me.

Jeanie Shaw
June 2001

The Big Picture

In love he predestined us to be adopted as his sons through Jesus Christ, in accordance with his pleasure and will.

Ephesians 1:5

One orphan—abandoned in the maternity ward. His caretakers are harsh and they slap him. He wears the same clothes all week. His shoes are several sizes too small. He doesn't get enough to eat. He shares his home with ninety other children. No one is there to hear his cry or to even care. Breakfast is stale bread and a little salami. Lunch is watery soup. Dinner is not enough. Occasionally he searches for extra food in trash barrels. One time he is so desperately hungry, he even tries to eat concrete!

Soon he will be moved to another orphanage for boys ages eight through twenty-four. They will demand that he beg and steal. If he refuses, they will beat him. Likely he will be sexually abused. He will never go to high school. He will be known as an orphan...nobody's child.

Then, seemingly from nowhere someone appears and says, "I want you. I love you. I long to care for you, to train you, to give you my name and my inheritance, to give you hope and a future. I want to laugh with you, cry with you and hold you when you are scared. I want to encourage you, tuck you in at night and give you a kiss.

"You will have a nice home, a great brother, two wonderful sisters and even two dogs. Outside your house across the street is a park with a soccer field, a playground and a tennis court. Your clothes are already bought for you and folded in your brand new dresser drawers. They are not hand-me-downs. You were carefully measured so they would fit you.

"There is a shiny new bicycle in the shed waiting for you. Your Christmas stocking still has candy in it from last Christmas when we only dreamed of your arrival. Your suitcase is already packed; I did it myself, just for you.

"The only thing you have to do is leave all you have and all you know and be willing to come with us. We purchased your tickets, filled out mountains of paperwork and spent a lot of money.

"Won't you please come let us love you and be our son?"

What should he do? What decision should he make? For us…from afar, seeing the "big picture," it is a "no-brainer." It is so clear from our perspective.

But…inside the walls of Casa de Copii Nr. 4, through the eyes of a young boy who only has known the "little picture," it is not so simple. *Can I trust these people? What I do have, I know; and it feels familiar and comfortable. I cannot even speak their language. I've never ventured beyond the few blocks around my home, and they want me to leave, go across the ocean…forever?*

For Jacob, this is a desperate struggle, an agonizing decision—one almost lost, except for the hope lingering inside him that there might be something more for him in life, something better…if he will let go of what he has always known.

We live our lives day to day so often in the little picture. The demand of jobs, the pursuit of money, the never-ending tug of tests, bills, laundry and you-fill-in-the-blank. While necessary, daily activities often call us to miss the *important* because of our focus on the *urgent*. The big picture consists of what is left when all these other things are gone. What will matter a hundred years from now? How does faith fit into the center of our busy lives?

Even though we are often confused and unfulfilled in our lives, we still want to hold on to what is known to us. We are fearful of letting go and trusting that God has something better for us. We hold to our own ways, even though time after time they don't work. From the little-picture perspective we are like abandoned children scrounging for our food in a trash barrel. The world can often feel cold, cruel and harsh like a big orphanage.

The adoption experience has helped me to see the big picture so much more clearly. I now long to know the breadth, depth, length and height of God's love and to grasp his hand and take this journey through life with him.

As an eager adoptive parent, God has packed our suitcases with exactly what we need, what is just right for us and what fits us perfectly. He is waiting with outstretched arms. He purchased our tickets and spent a lot of blood. All we have to do is be willing to go with him. It is so clear...when you see the big picture.

However, as it is written:

"No eye has seen,
    no ear has heard,
no mind has conceived
    what God has prepared for those who love him."
(1 Corinthians 2:9)

God Is Searching

"For the eyes of the LORD range throughout the earth to strengthen those whose hearts are fully committed to him."

2 Chronicles 16:9a

"So, how did you choose Jacob?"

The truth is we didn't really. God chose him for us more than six years ago when we first visited Bucharest. At that time, the country was still reeling from communism and a subsequent oppressive dictatorship. It was a very dark place. The scenes of hospitals and orphanages that we visited filled our minds, and we knew we wanted to help the children in many ways, including adopting an orphan. We began the adoption process, and almost one year later we received a referral for an eight-year-old boy named Andre. I planned to meet him on my next trip to Bucharest. Meanwhile, the orphanage workers told Andre that the Shaws would be his new parents.

When the day finally came to meet him for the first time, he had great difficulty connecting with me. He would not look at me; he did not want to be touched and could not sit still a moment. I had read about attachment problems, and I knew he would need a lot of help to overcome this deep need. This was a bit disconcerting, but I felt the lack of connection could be overcome with time.

Meanwhile, unknown to me, Jacob was watching me. Sometime that day, he decided that I should be his mother. He did everything to win my heart. He made it clear that he wanted to be loved by me: he followed me, smiled at me and strove to please me. That night I confided in my friend Roxanne the dilemma I felt because of being so drawn to Jacob. His tactics had worked like a charm!

"What am I going to do?" I implored.

We talked and prayed and agonized over the situation. I longed to adopt both boys, but I didn't really think that would go over very well with Wyndham. I begged God to provide an answer. I simply could not get brown-eyed, eager and lovable Jacob out of my mind or heart.

About a week later came a phone call: "Mrs. Shaw, I regret to inform you that you cannot adopt the child you had planned to adopt. I do not understand this. This never happens. But a Romanian family who first found him on the street has requested that he be moved to an orphanage near them as they plan to pursue his adoption."

Who would have ever thought of that solution? Only God.

So, we immediately began to pursue Jacob's adoption only to be told it was not possible. For some reason, his name was not on the international adoption list. He was older than a toddler at the time of the revolution in 1989, and it apparently was assumed by the government that he would be unwanted forever. He had never received an abandonment decree freeing him for adoption, and therefore he was not on the list of orphans. Though the lawyer who worked for the adoption agency searched over and over in the record books, there was no Iacob Nicolae. This name, Jacob's name, simply was not to be found.

During this time, our family had visited Bucharest, and Jacob had accompanied us to church. He had written his name on our daughter Melissa's notepad, spelling his last name "Niculae." Never before or since has anyone, including him, spelled it that way. I asked the lawyer to go back and check this spelling, and unbelievably, there he was. Jacob was on the list of orphans, and we could now pursue adopting him.

Jacob had certainly always wanted a family. But I later learned he did not "dream" of having a family. Orphans quit dreaming after a while...it simply hurts too much when the dreams don't come true. Jacob remembers people coming to the orphanage and looking at the children. He reasoned,

"They would not want me. My skin is too dark." I later learned that when the director and workers found out that Jacob was being adopted, they wondered why anyone would want him. That question is easily answered: it is because I love him.

It is often easy as adults to quit dreaming for our own lives. We get hurt and cannot seem to get beyond that hurt. We experience failure, and we get fearful of disappointment and disapproval. So we often try to stay "safe in our sameness." We feel defeated and unloved because the people we look to for help let us down. When circumstances go awry and God's timetable seems to differ from our own, we are tempted to lose heart or even become cynical. At times like this we feel forgotten.

But God never forgets us. He actively searches for us. People may forget us; circumstances may seem to be swallowing us into oblivion, but God will not forget us. He engraves us on the palms of his hands (Isaiah 49:16). God does not give up on us or quit dreaming for our lives. *We* are the ones who give up. *We* are the ones who quit dreaming.

I hope to always hold on to the fact that even though I am just an ordinary person, God reached out and found me. He adopted me as his own. He is always searching the earth to find those of us who desire a relationship with him, no matter how unlikely the choice may seem to us.

Why would he choose me? Because he loves me, and I want him to be my Dad. He has promised that if we seek him with all our hearts, we will find him. No matter the obstacles, we will find and know the Almighty God.

This is what the LORD says: "When seventy years are completed for Babylon, I will come to you and fulfill my gracious promise to bring you back to this place. For I know the plans I have for you," declares the LORD, "plans to prosper you and not to harm you, plans to give you hope and a future. Then you will call upon me and come and pray to me, and I will listen to you. You will seek me and find me when you seek me with all your heart. I will be found by you," declares the LORD, "and will bring you back from captivity. I will gather you from all the nations and places where I have banished you," declares the LORD, "and will bring you back to the place from which I carried you into exile." (Jeremiah 29:10-14)

Jacob's Shoes

"So in everything, do to others what you would have them do to you, for this sums up the Law and the Prophets."

Matthew 7:12

I stared at the feet of the two little boys in Wal-Mart. They looked about the size of Jacob.

"Excuse me sir," I asked the man who appeared to be their father, "could you please tell me what size shoes your boys wear?"

I had already been waiting for two years to adopt Jacob. I thought it would not be much longer. Of course, I had been thinking that same thought every day for the past year. It was therapeutic for me when the wait seemed unbearable to purchase a little something for Jacob to help me feel that having him would one day be a reality.

This day I decided to get him some sneakers. I proceeded to tell the story of Jacob to this stranger, and he was obviously moved. I talked about what Jacob was like and what it must be like to walk in his shoes. Each time I saw Jacob his little feet were stuffed into shoes far too small. This had gone on for years, and as a result, his toes were bent. One summer he at least had sandals...but they were huge, turquoise blue women's sandals. I cannot describe the sense of satisfaction I felt as I picked out those bright white "cool" sneakers.

I walked up to the register, and this stranger with his boys came up behind me with the same shoes I had picked out.

"Please, it is very important to me...I want to buy these shoes for your new son," he stated. I could see that he was determined, and tears ran down my face. I was so moved at his heart for this boy he did not know. His action reminded me how many people really do want to make a difference in this world in some small way.

It was soon time for a trip to Romania though, unfortunately, not the trip to bring Jacob home. However, I would get to see him. I remember so well the impact that packing those shoes made on me. I imagined how it would be to walk in them as Jacob walked—the places he would go, the people he would see, the thoughts that would go through his mind when he took them off at night.

When I arrived I was eager to give Jacob his new shoes; he was even more eager to receive them. He squeezed and tugged and managed somehow to get his foot mostly in. He had grown since I had last seen him. The shoes simply did not fit. He was trying to assure me that they fit, but it was not even close. I let him know I would get another pair for him, which was sort of okay, though very disappointing to both of us.

In Romanian he explained that he would like to give the shoes to Laurentiu, a young scrawny boy. He explained that the new shoes would mean a lot to him. It was Jacob's hope that when Laurentiu wore the new shoes, the kids would not pick on him so much.

After presenting this coveted gift to Laurentiu, we watched him walk with pride in every step and the biggest smile on his face.

I think of Laurentiu often. Today he is in an orphanage with all boys, up to twenty years of age. It hurts to think of him and things he must go through. What does it feel like to walk in *his* shoes?

The shoes the man bought for Jacob that day were size four. Now, two years later, his shoes are size eleven. His toes are no longer bent. I still sometimes study his shoes, and put my foot inside, just to think about what goes on in his head as he walks in those big shoes.

Jacob's shoes have taught me many things. Often, I don't really know what is going on in people's lives because I have not taken time to "walk in their shoes" with my mind and heart. I don't know what it is like to have no shoes to put on or to have no parents. I don't know what it is like to have been abandoned. I don't know what it is like to be sick for a very long time or to be physically challenged, to be very old and left with no immediate family. I don't know what it feels like to wonder where my next meal will come from or to be an outcast of society. It is easy to make assumptions that may not be accurate because of seeing things only from my own perspective.

Jesus had the ability to truly empathize with people while speaking the truth straight to their hearts. God knows us not only because he created us, but also because in Jesus God became flesh, put on our shoes and walked the paths of our lives. He not only knows every time we hurt or grieve; he hurts and grieves with us. Through his Holy Spirit he continues to "walk in our shoes."

> For we do not have a high priest who is unable to sympathize with our weaknesses, but we have one who has been tempted in every way, just as we are—yet was without sin. Let us then approach the throne of grace with confidence, so that we may receive mercy and find grace to help us in our time of need. (Hebrews 4:15-16)

It Doesn't
Make Sense

4

*And we know that in all things God works for the good of those
who love him, who have been called according to his purpose.*
Romans 8:28

"I don't understand, God! It is taking way too long. How
could it not be best for him to come now?"

This was my cry to God again and again during the long
wait for Jacob. In fact, the wait was so long that it actually
made history: Jacob's adoption took longer than any other
adoption in the history of the agency. Time after time it was
delayed, making no sense to me. For seven straight months his
abandonment decree was denied. No relative had ever come to
visit and none could be found, but he could not be officially
considered abandoned. It seemed that a judge's bad mood, an
"i" not dotted correctly or laws that changed from week to
week hindered the process. These delays caused me much
heartache and many tears. Sometimes I wanted to give up. It
seemed too hard. I could not understand. But I knew I might
never understand; I could only trust.

Today I understand more. In retrospect, the waiting period
does not seem nearly as long as it did at the time. Over those
three years we built a very close relationship with Ileana, the
lawyer for the agency. Because of changes in the law, the number of adoptions she could facilitate would decrease unless
she found an additional agency to work with. The director of
HOPE for Children was with us on the trip when we finally
came to get Jacob. As we signed the final paper for his adoption, the director and the lawyer signed papers to allow HOPE
for Children to begin adoptions in Romania three days from
that point. This goal had been pursued before, only to meet

many dead ends. This relationship also resulted in a partnership that allowed us to open the Saftica Family Center, a home for orphans run by HOPE *worldwide* New England.

On the day the adoption was finalized, Ileana, the lawyer who is now my close friend, told me that she and her sister Doina were discussing the long three-year wait. Even though they knew the wait had been agonizing for us, they also knew it had been a blessing for them and for many of the other orphans. Why? Because Jacob was such a blessing and a joy to them all. She saw the time of his adoption as the very best time because it was orchestrated by God for the good of the many.

Reflecting on what Ileana had told me, I thought of the fact that in the Old Testament Jacob became the father of many nations. I like to think that our Jacob was an encourager of many orphans who found happy homes and from whom "many nations" will be blessed in the future.

As I write this now I think of the twelve other Romanian orphans who have since been adopted into loving families. I also rejoice in the forty-one families who are in the process of adopting Romanian children through HOPE for Children. I thank God as I think about Ionela, Claudia, Alex, Ionut, Daniela, Gheorge, Marius, Ionel, Mariana, Ciprian, Marion, Nicoleta, Elena, Leonard, Alin, Cati and Florina who are now tucked into bed with a prayer each night in the Saftica Family Center. I think of what their lives would have been like without this home. This home would have never happened without the relationships built over the long three-year wait that had made no sense to me then.

When things don't make sense it is tempting to give up, get bitter or quit trying. I deeply admire Joseph, a man in the Bible who experienced many hard times and setbacks. He was a man who loved God and loved his family, yet his own brothers threw him into a pit and sold him into slavery. He held to his deep convictions about purity and righteousness, yet he was falsely accused of attempted rape. Though he was a faithful and responsible worker, he was put into prison and forgotten. Promises were made to him again and again and were not kept. One after another, people he counted on let him down. He often feared for his life. He could often have been tempted to reason that if his life circumstances were part of God's plan, then he wanted no part of this God. It would have seemed a very logical decision for him just to give up. How often he must have been tempted with bitterness and revenge.

However—Joseph did not give in to these temptations. He held on to what he knew to be true and right even when it made no sense to him. His conviction to trust God above himself was enough. He came to see that, through his difficult circumstances and his agonizing wait, God was working to bless others…a whole nation of others.

> But Joseph said to them, "Don't be afraid. Am I in the place of God? You intended to harm me, but God intended it for good to accomplish what is now being done, the saving of many lives. So then, don't be afraid. I will provide for you and your children." And he reassured them and spoke kindly to them. (Genesis 50:19-21)

What's in
a Name?

5

*Now it is God who makes both us and you stand firm in Christ.
He anointed us, set his seal of ownership on us, and put his
Spirit in our hearts as a deposit, guaranteeing what is to come.*
                                                    2 Corinthians 1:21-22

‘ **I** have something to show you," Doina said. She put a paper
in my hand. "This means everything," she explained.
There was a sense of wonder and excitement in her voice.

I did not know what to expect. The adoption process
includes a plethora of paperwork, so one more piece of paper
did not seem so special to me. There are applications, autobi-
ographies, home studies, crime checks, bank statements, doctor's forms, fingerprints, immigration forms, birth certificates,
marriage certificates and more. These must be notarized,
authenticated and sent around the world. The process itself
assures that adoption is something you have carefully considered. It is not easy.

So receiving another paper did not necessarily "fire me
up." I just wanted our new son. I just wanted to hug him,
clothe him, feed him, laugh with him, teach him...and above
all to know that he was ours, totally ours. I was not interested
in having another piece of paper.

Then I looked at the paper and realized why Doina would
say that "it means everything": it was a birth certificate, a very
special birth certificate. Under "name" it simply but profoundly
read "Jacob Shaw." That's it. These two words made all the
difference. It meant he really belonged to our family. No one
stood between us. This certificate was irrevocable. That word
is music to an adoptive parent's ears..."irrevocable." Nobody
could take him from us. We were responsible. It was signed
and sealed—a done deal. We would not turn back. Jacob
would have all rights, privileges and responsibilities of a Shaw.

He would have the inheritance of a Shaw. Our other three children were his siblings.

No nurse coached me to push; no doctor announced, "It's a boy," but this birth was just as wonderful and exhilarating as the other three. This paper was just as real, just as binding as the birth certificates that read "Melissa Allison Shaw," "Kristen Elizabeth Shaw" and "Samuel Wyndham Shaw."

Yes, I was thrilled beyond measure to have one more piece of paper. What doors it would unlock for a boy who had experienced door after door slamming in his face!

This was proof. Jacob was ours. He was, indeed, Jacob Shaw!

As an orphan in the universe (John 14:18), I longed to be adopted by my Father. I longed for him to hold me and love me and forgive me. I am so grateful that he gave me a way to be adopted into his family, a process of adoption that he clearly explained in his word. While this process does not test my intentions by requiring mounds of paperwork, it does reveal the depths of my desire to follow God. He tests my heart by requiring humility and repentance.

When I came out of the waters of baptism, God gave me something better than a paper in my hand. He put "his seal of ownership" on me and put his Spirit in my heart "as a deposit, guaranteeing what is to come" (2 Corinthians 1:22). And this means everything. It means I really belong to God. No one can stand between us. It is irrevocable. No one can snatch me out of God's hand, and he won't accidentally drop me. I would have to purposely let go and walk away. I have all rights, privileges and responsibilities of a child of God. He gives me the promised inheritance, eternal life.

I really don't think I can fathom, even now, the true significance of my adoption. All of God's family is now my family, my spiritual brothers and sisters. And God loved me and desired to adopt me into his family even more than I love and desire to adopt Jacob. Amazing…but true!

No, in all these things we are more than conquerors through him who loved us. For I am convinced that neither death nor life, neither angels nor demons, neither the present nor the future, nor any powers, neither height nor depth, nor anything else in all creation, will be able to separate us from the love of God that is in Christ Jesus our Lord. (Romans 8:37-39)

Counting the Cost

6

"I tell you the truth," Jesus replied, "no one who has left home or brothers or sisters or mother or father or children or fields for me and the gospel will fail to receive a hundred times as much in this present age (homes, brothers, sisters, mothers, children and fields—and with them, persecutions) and in the age to come, eternal life. But many who are first will be last, and the last first."

Mark 10:29-31

We had been to the embassy one last time. The whole adoption process was finished. Our flight home was scheduled for the next morning. It was now time for Jacob's good-bye party at the orphanage. We had cookies and drinks for everyone. Jacob gave each of his friends something they had asked for: watches that we brought from the States. We recorded a videotape of all the kids telling him good-bye so he could take it with him.

When the party was over, we were exhausted, but excited to grab up our bags and Jacob and head off to Pizza Hut. We started looking around for Jacob, but he was nowhere to be found. He had vanished. In all the commotion, he had slipped out of the room and had convinced the woman at the gate to the orphanage to allow him to leave. He had told her that he needed to tell his friends good-bye. Moved by his earnestness, she had let him go.

We knew he was feeling the emotions of actually leaving all his friends and the place where he had grown up. He was leaving everything he had ever known. He had a ticket to go to America early in the morning.

Pandemonium spread among the staff. The director was screaming at the woman at the gate for letting him go. The older kids and some of the workers ran out to search. Someone said, "Yes, the boy went toward the train. He was in a hurry."

I felt frozen inside. Sick to my stomach. *No God. It cannot end like this. He wants to come, I just know. We have prayed and prayed.* Time seemed to stand still. Two hours later, two of the longest hours of my life, one of the orphanage guards, who was also Jacob's personal friend, brought him back. What a glorious sight! I cannot describe in words the joy of seeing my son walk through that gate.

He had been found several blocks away, sitting on a bench in the park, his head in his hands. Truly, he was counting the cost. The idea of America and a family was fantastic. The reality of leaving was just plain hard. He was hurting deeply that his best friend, Marius, could not come with him.

He said to me, "Yes, I want to go, but I won't go without my friend. If he does not come to America, I must come back." We promised him that we would do everything in our power to find Marius a family too. (To God's glory, Marius should arrive in America in a few months. His new family, friends of ours, eagerly await him.)

My heart felt ripped in two. Yes, he needed some time and space to work it out in his heart. This was a forever commitment. He knew he would never live there again. Leaving was very, very hard for Jacob. Harder than I could have imagined. It was scary and took a lot of trust. I wished I could have made him understand what was waiting for him. But he was the one who had to trust enough to go.

Remembering the big picture is harder to do when you have never glimpsed the big picture. You just hope there is a big picture. Then you go to the edge of all the hope you can see and take one more step. That takes courage and faith.

I understand more than ever that in a moment's time for Jacob, after coming so far, all could have been lost because of fear and unwillingness to trust. Later I came to find out how much fear had been in Jacob. I had not understood it for so long. He had, after all, been familiar with us. We had always kept our word with him and showed him our love at every opportunity. However, during the time he was waiting to be adopted, jealous and misinformed caretakers and peers had told Jacob lie after lie: "They are adopting you to make you their slave." "When they bring you to America, they will slip drugs into your food."

These lies filled him with doubt, but when it came down to it, he was convinced of two things: we really did love him and being with us had to be better than staying where he was.

I thought about the ways Satan tries to tell us lies to keep us from following God's will for our lives. He often uses people around us to fill us with doubt and fear. They entice us to stay where we are. Sometimes it is because of their own jealousy; other times it is from simply being misinformed.

Jacob's courage inspires me. I know there can be no such thing as courage or faith unless fear is present. I have felt fear, yet when I trust God, he is always there on the other side of fear, waiting for me. I can be tempted, like Jacob, to run away from change or to procrastinate in letting go of the things that keep me from my journey with God.

That day in Romania, I felt only a fraction of the pain God feels when we run away from him. He waits for us with open arms. A decision to walk away is not just a bad decision. It causes the deepest of pain in the heart of God. All he wants to do is give us hope...hope that doesn't disappoint us.

Therefore, since we have been justified through faith, we have peace with God through our Lord Jesus Christ, through whom we have gained access by faith into this grace in which we now stand. And we rejoice in the hope of the glory of God. Not only so, but we also rejoice in our sufferings, because we know that suffering produces perseverance; perseverance, character; and character, hope. And hope does not disappoint us, because God has poured out his love into our hearts by the Holy Spirit, whom he has given us. (Romans 5:1-5)

God Will Provide

7

"Therefore I tell you, do not worry about your life, what you will eat or drink; or about your body, what you will wear. Is not life more important than food, and the body more important than clothes? Look at the birds of the air; they do not sow or reap or store away in barns, and yet your heavenly Father feeds them. Are you not much more valuable than they? Who of you by worrying can add a single hour to his life?"

Matthew 6:25-27

Sometimes the wait for Jacob to come home seemed unbearable. Every time the court was scheduled to meet to free Jacob for adoption, I would get my hopes way up...*This is going to be the day it happens. I just know it is.* After an unsuccessful day in court, Ileana, the lawyer, was always reluctant to call because she hated to give me bad news. Most times I would call her to find out the results. I could instantly tell in her voice that the wait would go on. Nothing new had happened.

I would then go outside, have a good cry and pour out my heart to God. I pleaded with him to help me understand why it was again delayed. For the first few moments after the telephone call, I wanted to be alone with God. Eventually one of my family members would find me outside and would hug me for a long time and usually cry with me.

During the long wait, I prayed so hard that God would take care of Jacob in a special way because I couldn't do it. I asked God to send someone to love him and prepare him for the future. I always liked to think that God had sent my little guy an angel. The evening before we left Romania to take Jacob home, I met her.

Jacob was back after running away (see chapter 6) and we were about to leave. As we walked down the path from the orphanage to the street corner, I noticed an elderly woman with a dog on a leash. She looked very worried…the lines in her forehead seemed intensified. Jacob stopped, petted the dog as he spoke to her and embraced the woman who seemed to not want to let go of him. Tears began pouring down her cheeks. We were introduced, and I learned that her name was Maria. She then embraced Wyndham and me and kissed our cheeks. Standing there on the sidewalk, she began to eagerly tell us her story through a translator.

Maria lives in a block apartment house behind the orphanage where Jacob grew up. She used to hear the children's screams and felt deep compassion for them. She watched their bony little arms stick through the gate begging for food. She longed to help in some way, so she started baking bread and taking it to the children.

At approximately the same time we started trying to adopt Jacob, she had managed to meet the director of the orphanage and asked to have some of the children come over to her home. She met Jacob and somehow felt that he was hers. She had him come over in the afternoons after school and allowed him to bring a friend or two with him. Though quite poor herself, she baked for them and often made them a meal. She became Jacob's "grandmother."

Once when Jacob did not come for a few days, she went to him in the orphanage and discovered he was ill. She brought him tea and aspirin. No details were too small for God to watch over. And all through those years, until the day of our departure with Jacob, I never knew Maria even existed.

As Jacob told her good-bye, I thanked God for what he had provided. I felt ashamed for my lack of trust. I thanked Maria for loving my son and I wept. God had answered my prayers in the form of a wonderful woman. From that day forward she called Wyndham and me her son and daughter. She left Jacob an envelope with two treasured family photos dated 1977 and the following note:

Dear Jacob,

I wish for you with all my heart a lot of love, health, and for God to take care of you, to keep you from all that is evil in life and to grow you in wisdom and give you a heart full of joy. My dear! I will miss you very much. I'll think about you all the time, but please I ask you never to forget me. I'm eager to hear news from you. My dear, please listen. Love what is right and all the time seek Jesus first, as he will be your friend and savior. May God bless you and your family. With joy, but also pain of your departure. Hugs and kisses.

Your Grandmother,
Maria

Jacob continues to call Maria each week. Here is another letter she wrote:

My dear Jacob and your family,
I got your letter and the photos on 19ᵗʰ of September. The joy was and still is for me as great as an explosion.
My dear child, do you remember when you were eating with me, how we thanked God and prayed for Him to be with you in your future. He, by his son, Jesus, heard our prayers and I thank Him. You do the same. Always be thankful, as I taught you. I pray continually for you and your dear family. I'm sorry I don't know English, but you'll learn for me, won't you.
My dear child, I'm still waiting for you; when the children are in the yard, I've the sensation that I hear your name. I miss you so much.
I'm very happy that God gave you such a good destiny, and I thank him for the phone calls and the letters, which fill in my life and soul. When you are older and able to understand, I'll tell you that you filled my soul when you visited me. Now that I have news from you, that Marius comes, I can say you are present, but in the rest of the time, I'm alone, with God and what he has for me. Now I look very often in the mailbox, because I have a family caring about me. The photos with you and your family are on

the table in the living room…Ursulina [Maria's dog] barks as if she would want to tell you something, and I wish you a lot of joy, success at school. Be a tidy and obedient boy and love your parents.

Love, Your Grandmother,
Maria

God had indeed sent an angel to watch over my son and to meet his needs.

God specializes in providing what we need when it can come from no one but him. I have read the story in Mark 6 countless times. Jesus, though very tired when he came upon a large crowd of people, had compassion on them and began to teach them. He did not want to send them away hungry. Even though there were five thousand of them and only five loaves of bread and two fish to be found among them, Jesus miraculously fed the entire crowd. He even had leftovers.

Often it is easy to be like the apostles and think that because we cannot see a solution for a seemingly impossible situation, there must not be one. However, we do not realize what God can do and is *doing* behind the scenes. He is at work when we do not even know it or understand it. He is at work when we see absolutely nothing by our own sight. He has always been able to make something from nothing. This is his specialty.

Jacob's Maria helps me personally grasp more fully that not only is God able to provide what we cannot, but he can take care of details. He does not provide barely enough. He provides enough for baskets of leftovers. Why then, do we worry?

They all ate and were satisfied, and the disciples picked up twelve basketfuls of broken pieces of bread and fish. The number of the men who had eaten was five thousand. (Mark 6:42-44)

Leaving the Past Behind

8

All of us have become like one who is unclean,
   and all our righteous acts are like filthy rags;
we all shrivel up like a leaf,
   and like the wind our sins sweep us away.
Yet, O LORD, you are our Father.
   We are the clay, you are the potter;
   we are all the work of your hand.

                                                        Isaiah 64:6, 8

Yesterday Jacob walked out of the orphanage for the last time and headed to our hotel with only the clothes on his back. That's it. He brought nothing. He owned nothing. There was no closet to clean out, no stuff to pack in boxes, no suitcases to fill. After his bath that night even the clothes on his back were left behind, tossed in a corner of a hotel room...across the ocean...never to be retrieved. They were soiled, too small and a bit like filthy rags. That's just the way it was.

Underneath was the boy I love. In place of those dirty, crumpled clothes in the corner of the room, Jacob received a suitcase full of brand new clothes that we had brought for him. The suitcase itself was pretty cool, and the clothes fit perfectly. He tried them on, and I must say he looked quite handsome. The next morning there was a different confidence in his stride—he knew he looked good. He was eager to carry his new bag himself. Everything about him showed that now he felt loved and cared for and special. He was wearing brand new clothes picked out by his sister, a teen with fashion knowledge.

I realize that what he was wearing really made no difference in the overall plan of life. However, I do know that he had never felt so clean, and he wanted nothing to do with the old clothes. He wanted to leave them behind. In fact, he did not even want them in his suitcase messing up the new clothes.

I loved the way I could see his confidence shine in his new attire. I knew that true confidence would grow from the inside out over time. But this was a great start.

How often in making a decision to follow Jesus we are tempted to pack our bags—lots of them! We can feel that our "old clothes" are pretty special and something we need to take with us. These old clothes can consist of a variety of things: past accomplishments, good deeds and other things from which we gained our security. It is tempting at times to wear these clothes because they can feel more comfortable than new clothing. We can even think in our pride that God is getting a pretty good deal to have us on his side and will be rather impressed with the nice clothing we bring. We fail to see that our own righteousness is nothing but filthy rags compared to the righteousness of God.

In actuality our old clothes are stained and torn. We "wear" bitterness, resentment, guilt, shame and broken relationships. When we pack these old clothes and try to take them with us in our journey with God, they weigh us down. When we stash the old in with the new it messes up everything in the bag. God wants us to throw our old clothing in the corner.

Jacob's dirty, crumpled clothing teaches me several lessons. There is nothing I can offer or bring to God to deserve his love. And there is nothing so repulsive about me that he will not love me. Also, I must get rid of my selfishness so I can have an "empty suitcase" to have room for the "new clothing" God has prepared for me. This clothing will fit perfectly and be exactly what I need. I am clothed with Christ and that allows me to walk day by day with confidence from the inside out.

I pray to learn this from Jacob. I need to leave all my baggage in a corner of the room, across the ocean…never to be retrieved…and then put on my new clothes and move on with confidence as God's adopted child.

> You are all sons of God through faith in Christ Jesus, for all of you who were baptized into Christ have clothed yourselves with Christ. There is neither Jew nor Greek, slave nor free, male nor female, for you are all one in Christ Jesus. If you belong to Christ, then you are Abraham's seed, and heirs according to the promise. (Galatians 3:26-29)

Anticipating the Journey

Brothers, I do not consider myself yet to have taken hold of it. But one thing I do: Forgetting what is behind and straining toward what is ahead, I press on toward the goal to win the prize for which God has called me heavenward in Christ Jesus.

Philippians 3:13-14

As I write this entry, we will be arriving in Boston in less than an hour. The flight attendants are tidying up the plane, and the travelers are sprucing up their appearances. A certain energy fills the cabin as we anticipate our arrival. I try to imagine what it will be like for Jacob to arrive in America. What will he first notice? What will he be thinking? Will he be afraid?

There are two ways to look at this moment. On one hand the long journey is over; on the other hand, when we land, the journey is just beginning. I have done extensive research and asked hundreds of questions, but all I really know is that the journey will be an adventure—one of laughter and tears, of great times and hard times. These adventures will be what make us family. I am grateful that we can begin this journey together, for no matter what it brings, I know those who are going with me...and their love makes all the difference.

The beginning of this journey already refreshes my heart. I see things through new eyes because everything is new to Jacob. On the plane he has not slept one moment because he has not wanted to miss anything. Or perhaps he is just scared. He doesn't know we are getting near his new home. He doesn't know when this flight will end and whether or not there is another one coming up. He has never done this before. The escalator at the London airport is as exciting as a roller coaster; a baggage cart is a race car; the food seems to never end. Toilet tissue is to be savored and touched, for it is a rare commodity.

A packaged hand wipe given out on the plane is like precious perfume—and the journey has only begun. We have not even touched down.

Too often, I believe, we let out a sigh of relief at the conclusion of an event, without understanding the timeline of the accompanying journey.

A death, a marriage, a birth, our own or someone else's baptism are often so in focus that we fail to prepare for what comes next. We see the "arrival" as the end of the journey rather than a new beginning. We often do not put the same anticipation and energy into the "daily" parts that follow the actual events. We can even get tired of the dailiness of it all and feel we should be finished; the challenges of the journey should be over.

In our marriages, do we help each other keep the love through the "poorer" times of "for richer or poorer" or the "sickness" side of "in sickness and health"? Do we learn all we can and get lots of advice in the years of parenting that follow the birth? Are we around to help someone adjust to the vast emptiness that settles in after the funeral is over? Do we help someone else grow and mature with as much eagerness and steadfastness as we did when preparing them for baptism? Do we put as much effort into our own learning and growth as we did when initially learning about God and how to please him?

These are all "touching down" or "landing" experiences that end one part of a journey and begin a new one. Our perspective on these experiences often determines how much we grow and how deeply we are able to love other people. How do you perceive your journey? Is it new each day, or are you at a dead end?

Do you not know?
    Have you not heard?
The LORD is the everlasting God,
    the Creator of the ends of the earth.
He will not grow tired or weary,
    and his understanding no one can fathom.
He gives strength to the weary
    and increases the power of the weak.
Even youths grow tired and weary,
    and young men stumble and fall;
but those who hope in the LORD
    will renew their strength.
They will soar on wings like eagles;
    they will run and not grow weary,
    they will walk and not be faint.
(Isaiah 40:28-31)

A Rich
Welcome

For if you do these things, you will never fall, and you will receive a rich welcome into the eternal kingdom of our Lord and Savior Jesus Christ.

2 Peter 1:10b-11

Butterflies fill my stomach. The wheels of the plane are down and landing is imminent. Though it is past midnight by Romanian time, where we awoke at 5:00 in the morning, Jacob insists that he is not sleepy. We communicate entirely by charades. He seems happy playing Sega and laughing at his dad's attempts at the game. He is on a long journey, having no idea where he will land. I have been telling him that soon we will be in Boston.

He asked, "Another airplane?"

"No, Jacob, you will be home."

You have no idea what planning and rejoicing has been in the works for your arrival and welcome. There will be a big crowd cheering and welcoming you home, young and old friends who for three years have been praying with us for you. There will be rejoicing, banners, balloons and gifts. Your brother and sisters will be waiting at the front of the line with outstretched arms. Your room is all set up for you. Your clothes are in your dresser, your shoes are neatly lined up in your closet, your bunk beds have new matching comforters and a huge stuffed bear is sitting on your pillow. Your new rollerblades and soccer ball are under your bed and there are banners over your doorway. How I have loved preparing it. It has helped to pass the time until you are actually in it. You have no idea of all of the preparation. Most of all, Jacob, we want you to know we are happy, very happy that you are home.

Home is a place Jacob has never been, but when he gets there, he will know that he has finally found where he belongs.

I can only imagine God, Jesus, the angels, Abraham, Gideon, Rebecca, Moses, Joshua, Timothy with his mom and grandmother, Ruth, Deborah and John, along with many others, celebrating, cheering and welcoming me: "We are glad you are finally home." I will come to a place I have never been, but when I get there, I will know that I have finally found where I belong.

There are people I can hardly wait to meet and others I long to be reunited with. I will love talking to Noah about life in the ark, especially being the animal lover I am. It will be such an honor to talk with men and women who went before me and faced persecution and martyrdom. I look forward to seeing the smiling faces of children who were dying before my eyes in the lonely hospital beds in Bucharest.

I know the care and precision with which I prepared Jacob's room. It is hard to fathom that God has prepared a place for me and knows just what will make me happiest. Not only has he put thought into it, but his full love as well. But most amazing of all…God himself will welcome me, embracing me with his mighty and loving arms.

> "Do not let your hearts be troubled. Trust in God; trust also in me. *In my Father's house are many rooms; if it were not so, I would have told you. I am going there to prepare a place for you.* And if I go and prepare a place for you, I will come back and take you to be with me that you also may be where I am. You know the way to the place where I am going." (John 14:1-4, emphasis added)

'Leessss Go!'

11

Then Caleb silenced the people before Moses and said, "We should go up and take possession of the land, for we can certainly do it."

Numbers 13:30

"Come on, let's go," he says with his thick Romanian accent, pulling me so hard I am afraid he might jerk my arm off. I believe this was Jacob's first English sentence, and it describes his character well.

I am inspired. Jacob has already gone fishing twice (once on the ocean); he caught nine fish and ate three of them for dinner. He has learned to ride a bike, and was so thrilled with this new accomplishment that he rode it until his hands were bleeding. He had an exciting water gun fight, joined a soccer team and has already practiced twice. This inspires me because he has only been in America for *four* days!

Yesterday at a cookout he watched the hamburgers sizzle on the grill, crammed one in his mouth and said his second full sentence in English, "Come on, hamburger!" He enjoyed it so much that he proceeded to eat three more burgers!

Today was his first day of school. He knew no one and possessed an English vocabulary of about twenty words. My stomach was in knots for him. I realized that he could not be sure I would come for him when school was over. He had no idea what to expect from school. I knew he was scared, though he did not show it. At the door to the classroom, he didn't hesitate. He simply embraced the challenge by saying, "Leessss go!" sliding the backpack on his back and walking right in.

I was so proud of him—he just put one foot after the other and went for it. He did not even consider the option of refusing something new and unknown to him. He is a young man of courage and determination.

How many opportunities and experiences do we miss because we don't approach them with a "leessss go" attitude? How often does hesitation cause us to become passive observers instead of active participants? It is this hesitant, passive posture that causes us to become critical of those who are not holding back, who give all they have. The more we hold back from participation, the more real our fear becomes; then it is easy to settle into complacency.

One of my favorite scenes in the Bible is when Caleb came back from spying out the Promised Land. He had full confidence that they could take it because he knew God was all powerful, and God was with them. Ten of the twelve spies did not see the possibilities; they saw only the huge people in the land. The ten did not look through eyes of faith, but Joshua and Caleb did. The huge people were small compared to God.

I am most inspired by the dogged determination of Jesus; he resolutely set his face toward his goal (Luke 9:51). He did not give in to fear of things he had not done before or places he had not been. He had never become flesh; he had never left his home in heaven where all was perfect. He had never experienced hatred, been alone or experienced death. He came to earth and most people he encountered rejected, mistreated and misunderstood him when all he wanted was what was best for them. Yet he never quit, even though it meant death, because he loved so much.

When I am tempted to hesitate, I think of him. I also think of Jacob holding his hamburger saying, "Come on, hamburger!" I picture him slinging his backpack over his shoulder and walking into the foreign fifth grade class saying, "Leessss go!" If this eleven-year-old can do it, why can't I? Young or old, this attitude is what keeps life—spiritual, emotional and physical—fresh and real.

> "I was forty years old when Moses the servant of the LORD sent me from Kadesh Barnea to explore the land. And I brought him back a report according to my convictions, but my brothers who went up with me made the hearts of the people melt with fear. I, however, followed the LORD my God wholeheartedly. So on that day Moses swore to me, 'The land on which your feet have walked will be your inheritance and that of your children forever, because you have followed the LORD my God wholeheartedly.'" (Joshua 14:7-9)

'I'm Good at Punch!'

12

Brothers, think of what you were when you were called. Not many of you were wise by human standards; not many were influential; not many were of noble birth. But God chose the foolish things of the world to shame the wise; God chose the weak things of the world to shame the strong. He chose the lowly things of this world and the despised things—and the things that are not—to nullify the things that are, so that no one may boast before him.

1 Corinthians 1:26-29

'I'm not good at math, not good at too much, but I'm good at punch!" These were Jacob's words as he tried to find a place to fit in. And not just fit in—but excel. He was trying to find something he could be good at. At the orphanage, he was strong and had big fists. He was a good fighter, and there were a lot of opportunities for practice. Working math problems did not come as easily as punching.

I want Jacob to be able to excel in something. However, there are many things going against him at school. He has a new language and a gap of several years of schooling that he missed as an orphan. He is, however, a good athlete, and he could excel in a strength sport like wrestling, karate or even football. (He desires to be the world champion in karate.) He wants to do something really well. When he is successful at something, his confidence grows. Confidence is hard for Jacob. As his brother and sisters excel in school and his brother excels in athletics, Jacob feels the difference in life experiences and opportunities. He senses that he is "behind" in so many areas.

Hopefully, he will get better at math. Because of his intelligence and ability to learn quickly, he should gradually catch up in school. Maybe he will be a star wrestler; maybe he will be world champion in karate. But then again, perhaps he will never "get" math, and he will just enjoy participating in his chosen sports. Maybe he'll be on a losing soccer team for yet another year, or maybe it will be a winning team. I have to remind myself that in the scheme of what is truly important, being the best at something does not really matter.

My prayer is that he will be a vital part of God's family and that he will learn the value of what he uniquely has to give. I pray also that he will realize how important he is to our family...whether he wins or loses a game...whether he passes or fails a test. And finally, I pray that he will learn to find confidence in trusting God in every area of his life. I hope to show him that he can never win love by being the best at something, but that he already has our love and God's love...and he always will.

Within each of us is a desperate desire to be valued, to accomplish something. We look for ways to be affirmed, to get noticed. If we can't get that affirmation from home, we will look for it most anywhere. We all want to belong and to feel important.

The world exerts great pressure on us to be champion athletes, to be smart, beautiful and rich. For many parents, success and competence in these areas are what they most desire and go after. Their children become an extension of the parents' values.

What does it mean then if someone can't be the best in these areas, or even among the best? Do they feel second rate, unneeded and of little value? I know when I do not feel good at something, I tend to lose heart and feel like "they" (whoever *they* might be) don't need me or want me. I believe this is true for everyone. It is vital to feel useful and important and to make others feel that way. However, misplaced values can mess us up in evaluating what really counts and what is really important. How many times did God take what seemed worthless, to teach us what is really important?

Perhaps as parents we can reevaluate the importance of the things our kids can excel in. Where do we affirm, give vision and blessings? Many of us encourage our children by saying things like the following: "Son, your making an A inspires me. I am so proud of you." "Your agility is amazing." "I will take you to the park today and throw the baseball with you." "I will get you a tutor in science." "I'll help you with your math."

These are good ways to help and build up our children. But we have to ask ourselves how often we say things like the following: "Son, your patience inspires me. I am so proud of you." "Your joy is amazing." "I will take you to the park today and throw the 'self-control' with you." "I will get you a tutor in faith." "I'll help you with your purity."

When our lives are over and we have done this or that, I long to hear, and long for Jacob to hear, the words from Matthew 25:21: "Well done, good and faithful servant! You have been faithful with a few things; I will put you in charge of many things. Come and share your master's happiness!"

Train yourself to be godly. For physical training is of some value, but godliness has value for all things, holding promise for both the present life and the life to come.

Don't let anyone look down on you because you are young, but set an example for the believers in speech, in life, in love, in faith and in purity. (1 Timothy 4:7b-8, 12)

'I Don't Know That Word'

Be completely humble and gentle; be patient, bearing with one another in love. Make every effort to keep the unity of the Spirit through the bond of peace.

Ephesians 4:2-3

It was late in the afternoon. The last hurrah of the sun's rays were filtering through the window. Jacob's arms were folded across his chest; his jaw set in firm determination. Wyndham was disciplining him for a really lousy attitude. He had actually been asking for it for a while with smug answers, mumbled responses, low-grade disrespect...and enough of the right actions to just get by. The focus of the attitude seemed to be on his brother, Sam, who was trying to help Jacob with his math.

"I don't need any help with math. Sam is not older than me. I am a teenager too," Jacob retorted. Certainly his vocabulary was expanding...as was his pride.

The facts were staring him in the face, but he was staring them back even harder. So what that his brother is—and always will be—three years older than he is. He was not going to concede that fact. Jacob had already admitted that he was not very good at math, but he was sure he did not need help...especially from his older brother.

We tried to recount the ways Jacob needed help from his brother. He needed rides, food, money, help with homework and on and on. Yet the response was still, "I don't need help." He changed the subject, blame-shifted and did all the usual acts of dodging the truth. It was so obvious to us. Yet he would not get humble.

Wyndham explained to him that he was not showing humility. After much talking on Wyndham's part and much stubbornness on Jacob's part, it was time for Jacob to go to his room and think about what his dad had said about humility and Jacob's need for more of it.

Jacob's reply was, "I don't know that word."

As he walked to his room, I thought...*Oh, he knows the word all right. He just doesn't like it.*

Here is a fact: The need for humility always seems obvious when someone else needs it. It is much harder to see when I am the one who needs more of it. There are many facts which tell me clearly that I need God and need other people. It is a fact that if God cuts off my oxygen, I will die. It is a fact that my judgment, left to itself, is dimmed by the blinders of my own point of view. It is a fact that sometimes I am physically unable to accomplish a task I have committed to do, and I need someone to help me. Funny, how it so often seems to come down to that one word for all of us...humility.

I know there are numbers of times it is hard to get out of our mouths the words "I am sorry" with no rebuttal attached. I can think of times I've given smug answers in my mind—I have had that same "lousy attitude" that Jacob had. However, through the years it gets easier to cover up such attitudes on the inside and to look great on the outside. I remember the Phillips' translation of 1 Peter 2:8: "They stumble at the Word of God, for in their hearts they are unwilling to obey it."

It is easy to stumble over meanings of words when we do not want to understand them, or when we do not want to change our personal attitudes or perspectives. It is easier to "not know that word" than to put that word into practice.

My dear brothers, take note of this: Everyone should be quick to listen, slow to speak and slow to become angry, for man's anger does not bring about the righteous life that God desires. Therefore, get rid of all moral filth and the evil that is so prevalent and humbly accept the word planted in you, which can save you.

Do not merely listen to the word, and so deceive yourselves. Do what it says. Anyone who listens to the word but does not do what it says is like a man who looks at his face in a mirror and, after looking at himself, goes away and immediately forgets what he looks like. But the man who looks intently into the perfect law that gives freedom, and continues to do this, not forgetting what he has heard, but doing it—he will be blessed in what he does. (James 1:19-25)

The Victory Is in the Hard Stuff

14

*This is how we know what love is: Jesus Christ laid down his
life for us. And we ought to lay down our lives for our brothers.
If anyone has material possessions and sees his brother in need
but has no pity on him, how can the love of God be in him?
Dear children, let us not love with words or tongue but with
actions and in truth.*

1 John 3:16-18

Anyone who has adopted a child knows that the victory is not
in the cute stuff; the victory is in going through the hard stuff.
We had some difficult days and weeks as Jacob adjusted to a
new country, a new language, a new family, a new home. There
were days when I thought, "Good grief, what have we done?"

The first few weeks Jacob would pack his bags each night
and state, "Good morning Romania," which we knew meant,
"I'm out of here." I expected him to be gone at any given
moment. In very broken English he would look at me and say,
"No I love you." He crossed out the name Shaw on everything
he had and rewrote his old name.

I remember a family devotional in which we were sharing
things we appreciated, and he could not find anything positive
to say. I tried hard not to take it personally and sought help
from a number of people who had worked with abandoned
children. One friend simply observed, "Sounds like Jacob is
really grieving."

Wait a minute, I thought to myself. He is giving *us* grief! It
seems I had failed to see the big picture. My friend reminded
me of the stages of grief: First, there is disorientation, shock
and denial. Then comes the bargaining. Jacob was a good bar-
gainer. Anger and depression usually follow, and Jacob had
a lot of anger inside. For many children it comes out in very
overt ways. However Jacob's anger was expressed more

through stubborn rebellion. This one was not fun. I'll get to the last stage—the stage of acceptance—later.

The anger and depression stage helped me remember to put my feet back in Jacob's shoes again. Eleven years of abandonment and institutions don't go away overnight. Leaving all you know doesn't either. Grief is real. It is hard to get through the hurt. It was going to take a lot of what my husband describes as "soaking an old, dry baseball glove in oil." It takes the soaking for the glove to become soft and pliable again. The more it lacks, the more it needs. I determined to be a "vat of oil" for Jacob that day.

Acceptance—the last stage of grieving—does come. The first real glimpse of this came a few months after Jacob's arrival. I remember being in a discussion with Wyndham and I had tears in my eyes. Jacob came into the room, saw my tears, and had a panicked look in his eyes. "Send back to Romania?" he questioned with great fear. Through all the threats to leave that he had made, I realized at that moment how much he loved us and wanted to be with us here.

Shortly afterwards, he looked at me and said, "Mom, thank you for adopting me into family Shaw." How sad it would have been for us and for him if we had quit when it was so hard and never crossed over into acceptance. Victory comes by pushing through the hard stuff.

I know unconditional love is what God had and has for me, so who am I to make my love conditional? It is when I am going through the worst situations that he "soaks me" in love the most. How willing am I to give the same love to someone else when in my mind it is least deserved?

It is so easy to want to quit when the going gets hard. Often we don't get the response we had hoped for, or changes don't come as fast as we would like for them to come. We get discouraged when we don't overcome sin and bad habits as fast as we thought we should. We can get tired of other people's sin and want to pull away. We get surprised when other people's "stuff" they are dealing with brings out "stuff" in us that we didn't know we had. Sometimes we get tired and don't allow God to strengthen us enough to push through. At other times the going gets hard and we get apathetic, lazy or fed up. I think about where I would be if Jesus had quit on me when it seemed too hard. But he did not. He loved me enough to never quit. He loved us all when we were unlovable. He loved without conditions.

You need to persevere so that when you have done the will of God, you will receive what he has promised. For in just a very little while,

"He who is coming will come and will not delay.
    But my righteous one will live by faith.
And if he shrinks back,
    I will not be pleased with him."

But we are not of those who shrink back and are destroyed, but of those who believe and are saved. (Hebrews 10:36-39)

Somewhere Out There

15

O God, you are my God,
  earnestly I seek you;
my soul thirsts for you,
  my body longs for you,
in a dry and weary land
  where there is no water.

Psalm 63:1

We had just finished working on homework, and I went upstairs as usual to kiss Jacob good night and say prayers with him. I realized my little boy has turned into a young man. His voice has deepened, and he has become quite strong. His weights for lifting rested by his bed alongside his karate uniform and the muscle shirt he won Saturday in the teens' "Iron Man Contest."

I turned to walk out, and nostalgia filled my soul as I heard a song playing on his radio. Tears ran down my cheeks as I thought about all that has happened to bring us together. I remember so well the nights I only dreamed about telling him good night and kissing his forehead. I marveled that he is actually here. Time goes by so swiftly. He was growing at such a rapid rate.

The song brought more memories of times I saw him scurrying to meet me at the gate of the orphanage. The kids would see me and yell, "Jacob, your mom is coming!" There would be hugs. It seemed like yesterday. Suddenly his muscles didn't seem so big anymore, and I realized he is still my little boy. The words to that song will always have special meaning to me:

Somewhere out there, beneath the pale moonlight
Someone's thinking of me and loving me tonight.
Somewhere out there, someone's saying a prayer
That we'll find one another in that big somewhere out there.

And even though I know how very far apart we are
It helps to think we might be wishing on the same bright star.
And when the night wind starts to sing its lonesome lullaby
It helps to think we're sleeping underneath the same big sky.

Somewhere out there if love can see us through
Then we'll be together
Somewhere out there
Out where dreams come true.[1]

This song is sung by a child and repeated by an adult. I would cry and sing to Jacob when I was on *this* side of the ocean and he was on the *other* side. At that time he was still sleeping in a cold orphanage with no one to tuck him in. I hoped he could hear me in his heart. I know he had never heard or sung this song, but I liked to imagine that he sang it back to me.

It strikes me that this song is something of what God might sing to me from heaven. His tender love sings out, hoping to be heard. He longs for me to sing back to him. Do you hear him singing to you? Would he find you thinking about him and longing to be with him? Is his presence real to you? Do you sing your response to him?

The distance between our house and Jacob's orphanage was immense. It takes almost ten hours of flying time just to get there. However, across the miles, Jacob was always on my mind and in my heart. I used to dream of the day we would finally be together. I imagined eating together with the entire family, going to the beach together and riding down the road together. I envisioned the day that seemed to take forever to come. Looking back, the waiting time now doesn't seem so

---

[1] Lyrics by Cynthia Weil, Barry Mann and James Horner, *An American Tail*, motion picture soundtrack, (Universal City, Calif.: MCA Records, 1986).

long; it actually seems irrelevant. I see more clearly how God feels toward me, and I am humbled that he waits for me. Because he lives in my heart, his presence seems—and is—very real.

When love is between us, the ocean seems only a small puddle; the orphanage and our home seem to occupy the same neighborhood. Love surpasses distance, and dreams still do come true. And God sings a love song for me...and for you.

> The LORD your God is with you,
>> he is mighty to save.
> He will take great delight in you,
>> he will quiet you with his love,
>> he will rejoice over you with singing. (Zephaniah 3:17)

'Be Careful My Passport'

16

But as for me, my feet had almost slipped;
I had nearly lost my foothold.
For I envied the arrogant
when I saw the prosperity of the wicked.
When I tried to understand all this,
it was oppressive to me
till I entered the sanctuary of God;
then I understood their final destiny.

Psalm 73:2-3, 16-17

During the first few months Jacob was with us, he constantly talked of going back to Romania. The language here was too hard, he missed his friends, and it all seemed difficult. He wanted to go back and live where things were familiar, and in his memory it felt easier. The grass seemed greener on the other side of the ocean. He seemed to forget the hunger, the loneliness, the cold, the neglect and all the negatives that went with orphanage living. I tried to help ease the pain by letting Jacob watch the videos of his friends and himself at the orphanage. Jacob would watch a few minutes and then turn it off. It seemed too painful to remember because he was here and not there. And right then, "there" seemed better than "here."

I was unsure of how Jacob would react when eleven months later our family returned to Romania with the HOPE Youth Corps. Would he want to stay? What would it be like for him?

As we approached Romania, Jacob's excitement grew. However, Bucharest looked very different to him this time. His orphanage had closed down; his friends had been distributed to various other orphanages, and the poverty was evident to him. The memory was much sweeter than the reality.

He needed to understand his past and have me understand it as much as possible. I loved meeting some of his friends and going to places familiar to him. It helped me know him and helped him feel known and connected. I will always remind him of his heritage and give him opportunities to speak his first language.

This trip brought closure for Jacob. It was good for him to realize more keenly where he had come from. He began to grasp how much had been given to him, and how much he had been spared. I smiled inwardly as throughout our two-week stay he often said, "Mom, be careful my passport." He wanted to make sure that he was going home with us where he now realized he belonged.

Jacob needed to remember the reality of his past. It helped him to not only be at peace with the present, but to remember where he had been.

Many times, after making an initial decision to follow God, we can ask ourselves, "What have I done? Life was much more familiar and comfortable before."

Jesus calls us to be humble, pure, forgiving and to put on qualities in our lives that are not our "first language." Looking through the eyes of Jesus is very different from our own perspective. It can seem to us like learning a foreign language. The instructions—to not retaliate, to be bold and courageous, to think of others as better than ourselves, to not be greedy—can seem as difficult to learn as reading *War and Peace* in a language totally unknown to us.

It is tiring to learn a foreign language, and it can tempt us to want to forget it and go back to what is more natural. Spiritually, we can too easily forget the guilt and lack of fulfillment that characterized the old life. We can forget the love of God that called us to a new life.

When the new, seemingly foreign, life of pleasing God seems too hard, remembering where we came from helps put it all in perspective. And please..."Be careful your passport."

But our citizenship is in heaven. And we eagerly await a Savior from there, the Lord Jesus Christ, who, by the power that enables him to bring everything under his control, will transform our lowly bodies so that they will be like his glorious body. (Philippians 3:20-21)

'It Takes Time, Dad'

17

Therefore, as God's chosen people, holy and dearly loved, clothe yourselves with compassion, kindness, humility, gentleness and patience. Bear with each other and forgive whatever grievances you may have against one another. Forgive as the Lord forgave you.

Colossians 3:12-13

In the day-to-day of life, sometimes it is hard to see the progress being made. At the time of this writing it has been nearly a year since Jacob became our son. At times, when he is frustrated with learning the language or experiencing new life emotions and concepts I tend to think, "Why is this so hard for you? Don't you get it yet?" Growth is such a daily thing that it is easy to not see the changes.

Then I remember that eleven months ago Jacob was five-and-a-half inches shorter, thirty-five pounds lighter and did not speak any English. He was unfamiliar with everything familiar to me. He had no idea what marriage was. He wondered why I did not kiss other men the same way I kissed Wyndham.

I often wish Jacob would share more of his feelings. I remember a special conversation last month when I asked him, "When you were afraid or just needed to know stuff, who did you talk to? Was there anyone?"

To this he replied, "No, I just talked to myself."

I see him struggle as he is dealing valiantly with his character. For instance, one day he came home and told me he wanted to "deck a kid" at school. He related, "Mom, I was so mad. Then, I told myself, 'Relax, Jacob. You're bigger than he is. Relax. Don't hit him.'" I was so proud of him.

I now see him rest his head on his brother's shoulder and gaze adoringly at his sisters. I realize that they have become tightly bonded. We help work through sibling squabbles and resolve them and realize, "This is good."

Wyndham is so good with the children, always drawing out their hearts. He was helping Jacob learn to express his fears, his love and to see that it was okay to cry. Jacob's response to his dad was, "It takes time, Dad. It takes time."

This past week we went back to Romania—Jacob's first trip back since being adopted. I realized how far he had come. People who had known Jacob before were shocked at his changes and his progress. More importantly, Jacob began to realize how far he had come. Often he had felt that he would never "get" English. Now he could do some translating for us.

Also, his heart had grown. It was big for his people. He was so eager to give Maria money that he had earned. He would proudly go to her house and slip forty dollars into her hand. Invariably, tears would roll down her cheeks; she would point to her heart, motion to me and give us both big hugs. He loved being able to give back in many ways something of what he had been given.

Learning to be patient does take time. It takes a lot of thought and a lot of energy. It means listening to what is being said and listening to what is not being said. It takes a lot of standing firm and a lot of giving grace. But don't we have to be patient with anyone we love? In fact, doesn't God practice extreme patience with you and me? I imagine there are plenty of times when God must look at me and wonder why I don't "get" it. Why is it so hard?

During the process of change it is easy to get frustrated. We want to be a finished product before we have been through the construction process. We want ourselves or someone we love to change at the snap of a finger. It is important to remember we are all under construction. Our children grew up singing a song with lyrics that went something like this:

Little by little and day by day
Little by little in every way
My Jesus is changing me….
Sometimes it's slow going
But there's a knowing
That someday perfect I will be.

Perhaps we are not yet where we wish we were. Perhaps people we love are not yet where we (and they) wish they were. The important question is, are we making progress? Along the way, it is important to see the progress…and it is good to enjoy the ride.

Now the Lord is the Spirit, and where the Spirit of the Lord is, there is freedom. And we, who with unveiled faces all reflect the Lord's glory, are being transformed into his likeness with ever-increasing glory, which comes from the Lord, who is the Spirit. (2 Corinthians 3:17-18)

Stones of
Remembrance

18

And Joshua set up at Gilgal the twelve stones they had taken out of the Jordan. He said to the Israelites, "In the future when your descendants ask their fathers, 'What do these stones mean?' tell them, 'Israel crossed the Jordan on dry ground.' For the LORD your God dried up the Jordan before you until you had crossed over. The LORD your God did to the Jordan just what he had done to the Red Sea when he dried it up before us until we had crossed over. He did this so that all the peoples of the earth might know that the hand of the LORD is powerful and so that you might always fear the LORD your God."

Joshua 4:20-24

Often when our family is together, we stroll down memory lane. We enjoy laughter and tears as we reminisce about the little and big incidents that bond us as a family. Jacob's entrance into memory lane begins much farther down the road, so we share family memories with him. I love to show him the pictures of the family before he came so he can understand our history as much as possible. I also love to pull out the pictures I took of him the first day we met. He was so small and had a head of long curly brown hair. (We call it his "big hair" picture.) He was sitting at his desk and wore a captivating smile. He still remembers the jacket I had on and reminds me when I wear it that I wore the red jacket when we first met.

All of our family pictures are stones of remembrance. They are small reminders of something much more important than simply what is seen. They tell of the relationships that we cherish.

Gordon and Theresa Ferguson have shared in Jacob's adoption experience in such a significant way. The Fergusons documented special moments on video: his arrival, first day at home, adoption ceremony and one-year adoption celebration. They have experienced along with us his day-to-day life. This represents more than their willingness to record events; behind the recording is their willingness and desire to share in his and our lives.

Jacob has not had many stones of remembrance that point him to family, love, security and being taken care of. It is often easy in the busyness of my days to fail to give him random acts of thoughtfulness and meaningful gestures of emotional connection. I have deep love in my heart, but I have to think about ways to make sure he feels it from me. Jacob does not often comment about these stones of remembrance, but I know they mean a lot to him.

Jacob's arrival in my life has taught me the importance of marking events, celebrating happenings and becoming more thoughtful. By nature I am a "fly by the seat of my pants" type of person who does not take the time to make people feel really special. On the other hand, Melissa, our oldest daughter, does this so well. She makes even busy events special and meaningful. She values relationships deeply. At the age of ten she was orchestrating the production of a Mother's Day video in which she and her six-year-old sister and four-year-old brother sang "Wind Beneath My Wings." That video is a treasure to me. In the midst of her high school graduation party, she presented Wyndham and me with a picture inscribed with the words to Celine Dion's song "Because You Loved Me." She then had a friend sing and dedicate that song to us. The afternoon before her wedding she took me to Walden Pond in Concord, Massachusetts, so we could pray together while we hiked around the pond. During these big events, it would have been easy for her to be caught up in her needs only. But because of her special displays of love and thoughtfulness (stones of remembrance), the relationship with my daughter became the focal point of these events for me.

It is also important during difficult times to show people in special ways that we love them. Several years ago Wyndham was gravely ill with pneumonia. On his worst day, our son, Sam, escaped a close brush with death. I had taken them both to the doctor that day, and because Wyndham looked so ill, little attention was paid to Sam who was quite ill as well. Later that night as Sam's fever spiked, I took him to the emergency room to find he had appendicitis—in fact, his appendix had ruptured before the earlier doctor's visit. He was immediately wheeled into surgery. I was feeling very lonely when in came my sister-in-law, Mary Ann, along with Kay McKean. My spirit was lifted. Kay had a little brown bag filled with plenty of sodas, water, cheese and crackers to last through the night. She didn't just leave the goodies; she stayed with me through the night as well. That little bag of crackers was more than a bag of crackers. It was a stone of remembrance. It was a symbol to me of a relationship that said, "I really care and I'm in this with you."

From the beginning God has given us "stones of remembrance." He has marked important events: after the creation he marked its finish with the Sabbath; after the flood he marked our safety with the rainbow; and after the crossing of the Jordan he asked the Israelites to mark the spot with twelve stones of remembrance. Jesus used fig trees, coins, fish, bread and wine to remind us of his relationship with us and the love that is behind the events. The greatest stones of remembrance were his pierced hands and feet and his spilled blood. Each week when we take communion we focus on these special stones of remembrance. We remember the relationship that is behind it all. God wants to make sure those he loves do not forget who he is and how much he loves us.

I realize many people lack stones of remembrance that tell them someone cares about them. We have the choice of loving people and offering them stones of remembrance or just going about life enjoying our own stones of remembrance. What kinds of stones of remembrance are you leaving behind?

When the LORD your God brings you into the land he swore to your fathers, to Abraham, Isaac and Jacob, to give you—a land with large, flourishing cities you did not build, houses filled with all kinds of good things you did not provide, wells you did not dig, and vineyards and olive groves you did not plant—then when you eat and are satisfied, be careful that you do not forget the LORD, who brought you out of Egypt, out of the land of slavery. (Deuteronomy 6:10-12)

Melissa's Story

19

And let us consider how we may spur one another on toward love and good deeds.

Hebrews 10:24

We were all sitting in the family room. I was dating Kevin at the time, and Jacob got a kick out of watching us together. He took our hands and pushed us together and told us to dance, and then he just stared at us with a huge grin on his face. Then, to my horror, as he was watching us, he asked Kevin why he had not bought me a ring yet. Of course, inside my head I was applauding my little brother, but publicly I was mortified at what had just come out of his mouth. Jacob saw we were in love, and it was just not logical to him that Kevin had not given me an engagement ring.

The next day, without my knowing it, Jacob got busy with a plan. He asked Dad if he could wash both of the cars to earn money. He spent hours vacuuming and scrubbing. With all of the money he had earned held tightly in his hand, he asked Dad to take him to the store. He was very determined and resolute about what he wanted to do with his hard-earned money. He searched until he found what he thought was the perfect gift: a silver ring with a heart that was studded with small crystals.

When I came in that night, Jacob was waiting on the front steps to give me his gift. Shyly, but proudly, he reached out his hand and placed the ring in mine. He had been so concerned for me that Kevin had not yet fulfilled his duty, and so he assumed the responsibility. That ring is absolutely now one of my most treasured possessions. At that moment my heart was completely bonded to this little boy who had become my brother.

I remember our family sitting around a table at a restaurant years ago as my parents first presented the idea of
adopting. This was long before we knew who Jacob was. The
idea was easily exciting and the decision seemed so simple.
How could we not offer our family to a child who had nothing
when my brother and sister and I had grown up with everything? When the child to adopt came to have a face—the face
of Jacob—the dream and mission to save this little boy was
powerful and inspiring to me. But the reality of bonding our
hearts was harder.

When he arrived home, I was in college two hours away,
soon to be married and living a very busy life. (By the way,
Kevin did give me a ring!) The idea of being emotionally close
to Jacob was exciting, but it did not "just happen." Memories
had to be made; friendship had to be built. He was now legally
my brother, but that title did not automatically make us close.

I had never really experienced Jacob's world before he
came to my world. I had visited the orphanage and gotten a
glimpse of where he lived, but I had never lived the kind of life
he lived. While at the orphanage, I saw for a few hours that his
clothes were worn, his shoes didn't fit, and he was obviously
underfed. I also saw a contagious smile that was his means of
communication, and huge, warm eyes and small dirty hands
that he grabbed mine with. It took time, effort and considera-
tion to make us close once he came home. But he was now my
brother, and I wanted him to feel like my brother and for me
to feel like his sister.

Jacob definitely was not going to be the one to initiate; he
simply had not been equipped to do so. I realized that if I
waited for him to reach out, we would never get close. I had
to figure out what he loved and then learn to love those things
with him. It has definitely taken me humbling myself to make
us close. For example, I am not the world's greatest volleyball
player, but Jacob appreciated that I tried to play with him. One
of our most bonding memories is of me trying to play, missing
the ball and Jacob literally falling on the ground laughing at

me. He enjoyed that spectacle thoroughly! My being very open with my "weaknesses" has endeared me to him.

We have also had some rather competitive bowling matches after school that made us laugh and connect with each other. I have definitely seen more karate and shark attack movies than I would have without him. These were not always my expectations of having fun, but they made him feel loved and special. That was fun to me.

When we think about God's church, the idea of having a family that is close and united is awesome, but making it a reality takes a lot of effort. It is easy to read John 13:34, and see it as a warm and fuzzy scripture: "A new command I give you: Love one another. As I have loved you, so you must love one another." I think that in actuality it is one of the most difficult commands in the Bible to obey. It is our obedience to this command, though, that most sets us apart from the world.

It is often easy for us to build our expectations of others from our own personal points of reference based on our experiences and emotions. We want people to initiate with us. On the other hand we do not make time to initiate with them because we feel we have "more important things" to do. We are willing to give only as much as someone gives back to us.

Humbling ourselves and opening up our feelings, hurts and weaknesses becomes too hard to do. We let people only so far into our hearts so that we stay protected. We fail to understand that relationships are what Jesus is all about and what really matter. I can often feel guilty and think I am not working hard enough if I take time to spend with my closest friends. Yet without relationships, my life does not really have impact, and I become busy...and empty. If we do not build "family," life is not fun, and people will not be attracted to

Jesus and his church because of our examples. When all is said and done, the memories I have with the people close to me are what count the most.

Building family also takes pulling in the people on the outskirts of life. It means learning to do what they love, and saying the little things that build them up. This takes more thought than time. It requires us to focus on how to encourage people and meet their needs. Loving, considerate words and actions go a long way in building "forever" bonds.

How much thought and focus do you put into your relationships?

> Be completely humble and gentle; be patient, bearing with one another in love. Make every effort to keep the unity of the Spirit through the bond of peace. There is one body and one Spirit— just as you were called to one hope when you were called—one Lord, one faith, one baptism; one God and Father of all, who is over all and through all and in all. (Ephesians 4:2-6)

Love Spreads

So Jesus is not ashamed to call them brothers. He says,
"I will declare your name to my brothers;
in the presence of the congregation I will sing your praises."
Hebrews 2:11b-12

A friend of my daughter Kristen was on a date with a boy for his prom at a school located more than an hour south of our home. This friend, Andrea, was listening to some of the conversations going on around her and noticed that some of the students were using phrases that Jacob often used: "Congratulation!" "You are my life." "I don't think so." They even spoke them with Jacob's distinctive accent.

"Do you know Jacob?" Andrea asked them incredulously. They turned to her and replied, "*You* know Jacob?"

"Yeah, I know Jacob. I talk to him all the time."

It turned out that friends of their friends knew someone at Kristen's school. They had picked up on Jacob's phrases and passed them on, accent and all, because they heard them from Kristen and thought they were so cute. The "Jacob language" had spread.

Kristen has a very special way about her. She is inspiring and passionate. She makes an impact wherever she goes because she gives wholeheartedly. She makes Jacob and everyone around her feel so believed in and loved. She constantly tells Jacob how adorable he is, kisses and hugs him and tells him that she could "eat him up." She tells her friends, classmates and teachers how wonderful he is, and she shares with them many of his endearing ways. People who know Kristen often find themselves falling in love with people she knows because of how she talks about them. And this was a perfect example—people an hour away from our home knew of Jacob and his cute phrases because Kristen had been speaking lovingly of him to others.

Jacob acts suave and cool, as if the praise and affection Kristen shows him doesn't really matter. I know better. He loves to hear it. He needs to hear it. When, because of her influence, he hears it from others, it makes him feel very loved and special.

People's confidence is multiplied when we spread praise and affection that we feel for them. Again, I asked myself a question: Do other people feel incredibly believed in and loved because of the words I say about them?

Nobody ever praised Jacob in the past, much less praised him in front of others. Instead they gave out accusations or just plain apathy. I fear there are a lot of *Jacobs* out there who would rise to the occasion if only someone would notice them and love them for the uniqueness with which they were created. They would love for someone to verbally take note of something they did well or to express appreciation for a quality they have. They would love to hear that they had been thought of and would love to be asked for their insights or opinions. I'm glad I learned this from my daughter.

I am reminded of the Samaritan woman, who caused her whole town to notice and admire Jesus because of the way she talked about him everywhere she went. It began when Jesus spoke to her at a well while she was drawing water. Jesus broke cultural barriers by speaking to a Samaritan woman. He spoke truthfully and lovingly to her in a way that changed her life and caused her to know that he was the Son of God. She didn't do it because she had to. It just happened as a result of her love and appreciation for who he was and what he meant to her. What kind of love for God and specific people do your words produce in others?

> Many of the Samaritans from that town believed in him because of the woman's testimony, "He told me everything I ever did." So when the Samaritans came to him, they urged him to stay with them, and he stayed two days. And because of his words many more became believers.
>
> They said to the woman, "We no longer believe just because of what you said; now we have heard for ourselves, and we know that this man really is the Savior of the world." (John 4:39-42)

Kristen's Perspective

21

> *"This is what the LORD says, he who made the earth, the LORD who formed it and established it—the LORD is his name: 'Call to me and I will answer you and tell you great and unsearchable things you do not know.'"*
>
> Jeremiah 33:2-3

Growing up, I always had the suspicion that my mom never really slept. She could hear me coughing through closed doors and down the hall. I was sure that she lay in her bed awake so she would be ready if any of her kids needed her—and I often did. I had many health problems throughout my childhood and into my adolescence. My illness caused a lot of pain, and many nights I would be awake vomiting. I had to miss a lot of school, and therefore my grades and my friendships at school suffered. I often felt that it was unfair that God had not given me good health. I felt that few people could understand how lonely I felt and how much pain I was experiencing. My teachers were often skeptical and unsympathetic, and my healthy friends did not want to wait until I got better to have their fun.

Although I felt that life seemed to be unfair at times, at home I felt very safe and taken care of. I could count on my dad renting my favorite movies and sometimes watching them with me while he rubbed my back. My mom somehow made the pain better while she sat with me and played with my hair. I always got straws with my cola, and she knew exactly how I liked my macaroni and cheese—extra soupy.

I am grateful for the things that I faced growing up. My health problems have taught me to have compassion for people and to give my heart to them completely. However, when my parents first talked about adopting, I wasn't ready to give my heart to a stranger, and I didn't feel compassionate. I didn't want to share my home and the love that my parents had for me. I felt very possessive of my home and the security it offered. It wasn't until I visited the orphanage and saw the suffering of the innocent children that I realized how much I had and needed to give.

Jacob has been my brother for three years now, and I can't picture my family without him. He is very special to me. I was with him for a year before I left for college, and now each time I come home I make sure I make up for all of the kisses and hugs I missed while being away. When I think about Jacob, and how for so many years he had no one to call to when he was sick, no one to bring him his favorite drink with a special straw, no one to rub his back or comfort him with soothing words, my heart breaks. He has given me a new perspective on what it means to be lonely and to feel that people don't under-stand. I will never know what it feels like to have given up on crying or asking for help because no one would come to wipe away my tears or give me the help that I needed.

Today, although Jacob still has trouble asking for help, he is learning that he will be taken care of. His soccer team recently won the division championship, and he had a great game, scoring two goals. As we walked back to the car, he said he felt a little dizzy but did not make a big deal of it. When we came home his temperature was 104 degrees, and we found out later that he had strep throat. Although he was not aware of it, I am sure that our mom slept with one eye open listening for her son, waiting to take care of whatever he needed.

God, in much the same way, is waiting for us to call to him so that he can take care of our needs. So often we can look at the challenges placed before us and get angry or bitter toward

God. Often when I was sick, I lay in bed and struggled for understanding. At times I got angry. We can think that God is unfair, and yet he may be trying to get us to ask him for help. Through my hard times he protected me and taught me so many things that I have been able to use to help others.

He provides us with so much that we often overlook. Jeremiah 29:11-13 talks of the plans that God has for us—all we have to do is seek him wholeheartedly. I have sometimes wondered why God would allow Jacob to have grown up so alone, and yet now I know that God has had a perfect plan for Jacob all along. I am confident that one day Jacob will be able to help and relate to people in a special and unique way. God puts all different kinds of challenges in our lives to help us in one way or another. We have to be patient and submit to God's perfect and prosperous plan.

"Behold, I will create
    new heavens and a new earth.
The former things will not be remembered,
    nor will they come to mind.
They will not toil in vain
    or bear children doomed to misfortune;
for they will be a people blessed by the LORD,
    they and their descendants with them.
Before they call I will answer;
    while they are still speaking I will hear."
(Isaiah 65:17, 23-24)

'Sam No Pajamas, Me No Pajamas'

22

> Command and teach these things. Don't let anyone look down on you because you are young, but set an example for the believers in speech, in life, in love, in faith and in purity. Until I come, devote yourself to the public reading of Scripture, to preaching and to teaching. Do not neglect your gift, which was given you through a prophetic message when the body of elders laid their hands on you.
>
> Be diligent in these matters; give yourself wholly to them, so that everyone may see your progress.
>
> 1 Timothy 4:11-15

He carried his little bundle proudly as he stepped onto the bus with the rest of the HOPE Youth Corps volunteers. We were taking the group on a retreat in the beautiful mountains of Romania and had been given permission from the orphanage director to take Jacob with us. His little bundle contained a pair of socks, a jacket and some blue pajamas. Jacob would be staying in a hotel room for the very first time and would be rooming with his future big brother, Sam. Jacob had taken to Sam ever since he had seen him the previous year, and was excited now that he could get to be with him "up close and personal." He and Jacob spent some great time together. That night the whole family went to their room so we could tuck Jacob in and say prayers with him as a family. I remember how happy Jacob looked and how cute he looked in his stretchy blue pajamas that fit him quite snugly.

The next day was equally fun filled, and again we gathered that night as a family in Sam and Jacob's room. As I was communicating with him through our use of charades to get ready for bed, he looked at me with his hands on his hips and said, "Sam no pajamas, me no pajamas!" So that night Jacob slept in his shorts, just like Sam.

I began to realize at that point just how important Sam's role was going to be in our adoption of Jacob. He wanted to be just like Sam, and still does. Nothing could make me happier than for Jacob to follow the lead of his brother in his example of heart and attitude. Jacob needed a hero who was ahead of him, but close enough in age so he would be able to emulate and imitate him.

It was sobering and flattering to Sam to be looked to so intently, and he has taken on the role of hero and mentor in a great way. Sam has a maturity and spirituality beyond his years, yet he keeps us laughing all the time with his humor. Now that Jacob is here, he and Jacob are a comedy team. Sam plays many sports, and that has also spurred Jacob on as they have a lot of friendly, yet sometimes fierce, competition. Through it all, I am aware that Jacob deeply admires his brother and wants to be like him.

God longs for us to read the Scriptures and learn about how to live a life that is pleasing to him. But we also need relationships with people who are flesh and blood examples to help us along the way. That is why he put us in his family, the church. Many of us are like Jacob—we need someone to look up to. We have come from life situations where we have never seen marriage work, have never experienced peaceable conflict resolution, have never received or spoken words that build up. Many of us are like Sam—we are always being watched and are showing someone how to live the life of a disciple in a day-by-day way. We will define for many people what a disciple truly is by how we live our lives.

I could tell of so many people who have been heroes to me and taught me so many practical and deeply spiritual things. I realize the importance of my own example when people tell my daughters that they remind them of me. We are all examples, one way or another.

I am so grateful for the men and women of faith recorded in the Bible, many of whom experienced great persecution and even martyrdom. We are instructed to imitate their faith and consider the outcome of their lives. They lived their lives with confidence, peace and purpose, and continually made a difference in the lives of those they touched.

So, all of us need people to inspire us and point us to Jesus. We also need to take on the challenge of being an inspiration for others. For each of us, some person is watching and saying, "You no pajamas, me no pajamas."

> Remember your leaders, who spoke the word of God to you. Consider the outcome of their way of life and imitate their faith. Jesus Christ is the same yesterday and today and forever. (Hebrews 13:7-8)

Sam Speaks

23

We love because he first loved us. If anyone says, "I love God," yet hates his brother, he is a liar. For anyone who does not love his brother, whom he has seen, cannot love God, whom he has not seen. And he has given us this command: Whoever loves God must also love his brother.

1 John 4:19-21

"You have something to do? Can you do something with me?" These are the two typical questions I hear from Jacob when I walk in the door after school, football practice or hanging out with my friends. Being Jacob's brother and the closest to his age in the family, my relationship with him is different from his relationship with the others. As we have bonded through the things that teenage boys do—playing, laughing and joking—he has become more comfortable with talking to me about the serious side of life. We have shared some very special times. Opening up our hearts has allowed us to become brothers who are also friends.

One of Jacob's favorite things to do is to take walks. During one of our walks together, I began to ask him a few questions about his life in the orphanage. He talked about disturbing things such as having to wear the same smelly clothes every day or being hit by the workers. He then went on to say that there were many worse things than that, but he didn't know how to explain it in English. Then he told me something that I'll always remember. He said that he wished he could show me a movie of all the things he had to go through in the orphanage because then I would be able to understand him better.

There have been many times in my relationship with Jacob when I have lost sight of the life he came from. Because of sports and other responsibilities, I'm not always able to spend the amount of time with him that he wants. In a few months I will begin college and will no longer live at home. I realize that the time I have left at home is short. Thinking of this brings on many emotions and memories, and causes me to want to make the absolute most out of the remaining time with Jacob.

I think about what life would be without Jacob. Sure, it would be easier—I wouldn't have to get out of my comfort zone nearly so often. However, I would have missed out on a relationship so very valuable to me, one full of a lot of fun and a lot of challenges. I am a better person because of Jacob. I can barely remember what it was like before he came because he is such a part of my life. He is family. It's hard to imagine coming home and not hearing a new, creative nickname for me that Jacob has come up with.

When Jacob feels like I'm not being the big brother he wants me to be, his past doesn't teach him to talk to me about it with a forgiving heart. Instead, he gets mad at me and says things that hurt me in order to get back at me for how I hurt him. During these times, I can get angry with Jacob for treating me the way he does. Rather than understanding his inability to deal with being hurt, I can focus on my own hurt and resulting anger, and then I pull away from him even more. This makes Jacob feel unloved, and he makes a comment such as, "I have no brother" or a sarcastic comment such as, "*Nice* brother I have." These things cut my heart and cause me to re-evaluate what it means to be a brother and what it means to love.

God has taught me so many things that have helped me overcome this weakness of pulling back my heart. I realized my love for Jacob was too conditional. I expected Jacob to deal with his feelings the way I had been taught through the Bible and the help of my parents. There is no way I can expect that of Jacob. He received no Biblical guidance in the orphanage.

He had no one who loved him or who taught him what was right and wrong. I had to understand this.

The only way I was truly able to change my heart toward Jacob was through seeing the unconditional love that God has for me. Every day I do something that disappoints God or isn't what he expects from me. There are times when I choose to meet my own needs above someone else's needs. Sometimes I can let fear keep me from speaking boldly to others about God. Yet, he never pulls away from me or says that I don't deserve his love. My definition of love was not even close to the true definition of love: God's love. The more I understand God's unconditional love for me, the more my life changes. His love for me has brought my love for Jacob to a new level. He is my brother. He is my friend, and I love him.

> You see, at just the right time, when we were still powerless, Christ died for the ungodly. Very rarely will anyone die for a righteous man, though for a good man someone might possibly dare to die. But God demonstrates his own love for us in this: While we were still sinners, Christ died for us. (Romans 5:6-8)

Iron Man

24

I will give you a new heart and put a new spirit in you; I will remove from you your heart of stone and give you a heart of flesh.

Ezekiel 36:26

When God handed out muscles, he was generous to Jacob. His forearms are like two of mine. His hands are like hams. He is the only thirteen-year-old kid I know with an abdominal "six pack." He saved up some of his money, and instead of buying video games as many boys his age would, he bought an "ab" machine. He keeps some weights by his bed because he really enjoys working out. He feels confident in this area, and it is fun for him. I can't relate to it, but I appreciate it.

Recently Wyndham was wrestling around with him and commented on Jacob's strong muscles. Then he said, "Jacob, your arm muscles are strong, but your 'emotional muscles' are tiny little muscles...itsy-bitsy little things." They laughed about it, but his dad went on to explain. He told him how God had given him physical muscles and feeling muscles but that he needed to "exercise and work out" with those feeling muscles.

Jacob doesn't cry. It is difficult for him to express hurt or disappointments. He is an emotional being because he is created in God's image. However, years of hurts, disappointments and a lack of nurturing caused him to put a shell around his heart. It is gradually softening, but the emotional part of him needs a personal trainer. He grew up never verbalizing his emotions. He must now be convinced that to be close to people and to be more complete as an individual, he has to learn yet another foreign language—the language of feelings.

I always knew my family loved me. Jacob, however, never had that privilege until three years ago. He needs a lot of personal trainers. The training comes in many ways. When we tell him we love him, we don't leave until he says it back. When we hug him, we ask for his arms to wrap around us. We try to nurture a safe environment of trust and initiate the "heart" talks.

Sometimes he asks, "Why do you ask me these things?" I reply, "Because I love you and I want to know you." The weight of the emotional bar Jacob is able to lift is still light, but he is growing stronger. I know in the future that he will grow in his ability to express and feel emotions because he is making the effort and has many personal trainers. We are helping him and he is asking God to help him. He is learning how other men express their heart by listening to some of David's psalms and by hearing his dad pray. I believe that one day he will become a man able to express his heart very well. He will become not the Iron Man, but a man of "steel and velvet." Then, like David, he will be a "man after God's own heart."

Jacob is not the only one who needs to build up his feeling muscles. Fears, insecurity and past failures have caused many of us to put a shell around our hearts. At some point we decided that it was too difficult to be open and vulnerable. So we got good at stuffing things. This resulted in our being hardened to our emotions.

Deciding to be open and vulnerable is a very hard thing to do. I always thought I was an easy person to know and be close to until some friends told me that they found it difficult to feel close to me. They said that I did not express my need for other people and was not vulnerable and open. It took a while for me to understand this. I was open with my husband, because I felt that he was a "safe place," and I fully trusted him. I realized how much mistrust and fear I had for people and how much I had been stuffing my feelings. I tried so hard to be a "good person" who "did the right thing" that I became an unrelatable person who was quite out of touch with what I really thought. I came to a conviction that when I did not express the doubts, fears and hurt feelings that were in my mind, I was being dishonest. I realized that when others did not feel that I needed them, it was because I had built an independent little world. While I wanted to change these things, my emotional muscles were atrophied. I had to decide to trust.

In several situations in my past I had said things that were on my heart and they came crashing back down on my head. One time it even resulted in my husband being fired from a preaching job in a traditional church that was not practicing the Bible. Once I decided to trust, I learned that my church family now was a very safe place because these brothers and sisters had decided to hold to Biblical truths. I had to deliberately practice being honest and vulnerable, and I shared with others around me that I was working on this area of my character. I asked them to help me and to tell me if they felt I was not being vulnerable. This was hard and took deliberate training each day. I believed 2 Corinthians 12:9 that states, "But he said to me, 'My grace is sufficient for you, for my power is made perfect in weakness.'"

I am thrilled when others tell me how much my vulnerability helps them. I thought the day I would hear that would never come. I still have to remember to exercise my heart and to be open, but it is an exercise well worth the effort.

> We have spoken freely to you, Corinthians, and opened wide our hearts to you. We are not withholding our affection from you, but you are withholding yours from us. As a fair exchange —I speak as to my children—open wide your hearts also. (2 Corinthians 6:11-13)

'Don't Forget Me'

"Do not let your hearts be troubled. Trust in God; trust also in me. In my Father's house are many rooms; if it were not so, I would have told you. I am going there to prepare a place for you. And if I go and prepare a place for you, I will come back and take you to be with me that you also may be where I am."

John 14:1-3

'Don't forget to pick me up," Jacob instructed as I dropped him off for his Bible class. He loves his class, and yet I noticed that he repeated this phrase, "Don't forget to pick me up," about six times before he actually went into the room. I really did not realize it until this morning, but as I think about it he usually says this several times at the door of his class.

"I won't forget to pick you up. Have I ever forgotten to pick you up, Jacob?" He knows the answer is no, although one time after a meeting I drove off, not realizing he was not in the car. He was with one of my friends, and I realized it quickly and hurried back. For Jacob, the fear of being forgotten is ingrained in his heart. When he was an infant his biological mother dropped him off and never picked him up—and never will. I try to tell him that I am sure in her heart of hearts she loved him. In Romania times were and are so hard there is often desperation in women who cannot care for their children. At least they often take them to a place where they hope they will be cared for. But Jacob at this point in his life can only see her action as meaning that she didn't love him.

Sometimes I am amazed that Jacob is willing to learn to trust. While we were in the process of adopting him, for three years all we could tell him was that we were adopting him as fast as we could. Though we saw him about twice a year, I know he must have doubted and been disappointed time after time. He really had no reason to trust because so many around him were untrustworthy. The adult workers would even steal the gifts we sent him. I asked Jacob often if the waiting was discouraging him. His reply still rings in my ears: "You have said you will come for me, so you will come." We had never lied to Jacob and we were his first ray of hope. The decision to trust began, and he allowed himself to be vulnerable.

I realize with Jacob again and again that trust must be built. People all around him for eleven years were not trustworthy. I want Jacob to always be secure and able to trust me. When we travel, or just when I am not home for a few minutes after school, it takes extra thought to make sure that he feels my love and presence. It is very important to him to know all the details of his schedule and who will be with him. I can't just say, "See you later. I'll be back."

He is very aware of words and promises, and if I do not follow through with my words it hurts his trust and sets it back. I try very hard to follow through precisely on everything I say, no matter what it is, but I realize I don't always do it perfectly or wholeheartedly. If my heart is not there, he picks it up immediately. He seems to have an extra-sensitive radar to the integrity of words and promises. Knowing that helps me be careful in what I say and how I say it.

Jacob is not the only one who has radar for feeling loved...most people do. Some are more sensitive than others. If I quickly pass by and speak to someone without really connecting—they know it. If I don't call back or work at making others around me feel remembered—it hurts their trust. The more disappointments they have had with life, the keener they feel a slight from me. More often than I wish, I get caught up in busyness and therefore neglect the connections that help people build trust in my care and concern for them.

I am amazed at Jesus. He was resolute in his purpose, yet sensitive enough to feel power go out of him when a woman in need touched his cloak. Glances he gave, whether to the rich young ruler or to Peter after his betrayal, touched people to the core of their being. He remembered people's needs, even as he was hanging on the cross. He met his disciples after his resurrection with breakfast cooking on the shore. He does not forget me. Jesus' promises and words are ones I can always count on.

This is what I appreciate perhaps the most about Jesus—he has always kept his promises, and he will never leave me or forget me.

> He remembers his covenant forever,
>   the word he commanded, for a thousand generations,
> the covenant he made with Abraham,
>   the oath he swore to Isaac.
> He confirmed it to Jacob as a decree,
>   to Israel as an everlasting covenant. (Psalm 105:8-10)

Things Aren't Always As They Seem

26

"In them is fulfilled the prophecy of Isaiah:

"'You will be ever hearing but never understanding;
you will be ever seeing but never perceiving.
For this people's heart has become calloused;
they hardly hear with their ears,
and they have closed their eyes.
Otherwise they might see with their eyes,
hear with their ears,
understand with their hearts
and turn, and I would heal them.'"

Matthew 13:14-15

'So, how's it going?"

This a question I ask the kids when we are away on business and I call home. Being out of town has always been emotionally hard for me because I don't like being away from the kids. Things always seem to happen, whether it is sickness, baseballs through windows, love traumas or even great awards. However, I know the children are in good hands, and without the travel we have done, we would not even have Jacob.

"Things are going well, Mom. We are all doing well. Oh yes...Jacob almost got arrested today."

"Hello, excuse me!"

That day, Jacob had called "911" just to see what would happen. He did not understand the implications or that the police would come. I can just imagine his eyes when he opened the front door and saw a policeman standing on the porch. I think he learned his lesson.

One day, after being here several months, he was with Kristen and told a good friend who was an adult to "shut up." Kristen was horrified, and he later called our friend and apologized To the older three kids, these actions were unthinkable. They had not been raised like that. Not that they were always the pictures of innocence…it's just that their background and the things they struggled through were very different from Jacob's. He had grown up surviving by stealing food and smoking cigarette butts. These background differences often cause Jacob to see things from a different perspective than the other kids do. Once when I asked Jacob what his favorite orphanage memory was, he said, "Stealing with Marius. We were hungry and wanted food. The candy was wonderful!"

I thought back to the last day of fifth grade for Jacob. He had had a good year, but on the last day he had to go to the principal's office. He had heard a boy swearing, and the phrase included the word "mother." Jacob took this very personally and grabbed the boy's collar, looked in his face and said, "No one talks about my mother that way." Fortunately, the principal took time to understand Jacob, and explained that the boy was doing something wrong, but was not talking about Jacob's mother.

Words, when not understood, can be confusing and cause reactions because we don't stop to find out what is meant. One day, I was explaining to Jacob how much I loved him. He asked, "Will you love me next day, and next?" to which I replied, "Jacob, I will love you always."

He had the most troubled expression on his face and finally asked, "Why you love me girl's stuff?" You see, Jacob often went to the grocery store with me and studied all the products that line the shelves. "Always" to him meant the package of sanitary products for women. What was an expression of unending devotion to me was a seeming insult to him. It takes careful listening to hear with another's ears and understand with another's heart.

Often I think it is hard to understand someone else's actions because we are looking at them from the shores of *our* experiences. Whether it is between a husband and wife, parent and child, or just friends, we can miss what the other person is really saying because we are not trying to hear from their point of view. We get so caught up in the emotions of our response that we do not truly listen. When something doesn't sit well with us in a conversation, do we make quick assumptions or do we ask questions to clarify what the other person is saying? Do we state what we are hearing and ask if that is the intended message? If not, we may end up "at war" in our words, hurting one another because we were not quick to listen and slow to speak.

In Joshua 22, two peoples almost went to war because of assuming that the way they saw something was the way it actually was. I love this story and try to remember it often. Please take time to read the account. It is a strong reminder to the importance of true listening without assuming. I'm glad Jacob asked his question. It reminded me to listen more carefully. How often we miss one another because we are standing on the opposite shore and don't ask the questions.

My dear brothers, take note of this: Everyone should be quick to listen, slow to speak and slow to become angry. (James 1:19)

'Who's the Big Guy Here?'

For the word of God is living and active. Sharper than any double-edged sword, it penetrates even to dividing soul and spirit, joints and marrow; it judges the thoughts and attitudes of the heart. Nothing in all creation is hidden from God's sight. Everything is uncovered and laid bare before the eyes of him to whom we must give account.

Hebrews 4:12-13

Jacob is a "bottom line" kind of guy. He does not readily accept things at face value but wants to know the purpose behind them. For instance, when we first prayed before a meal, he wanted to know why we did that. His questions cause me to re-evaluate why I do what I do.

When in group situations Jacob will often ask, "Who's the big guy here? I mean the big, big guy?" Jacob realizes that in everything there is ultimately someone in charge, someone who has the final word. It makes sense to him that if he knows who is over it all, he can figure out how he should live in any given arena. He then knows who is the most important person to please.

I remember being on a large bus in Romania with the teens from HOPE Youth Corps. Wyndham and I were sitting with several adults when the bus driver stepped onto the bus. Jacob looked around, as if scoping out the situation. He looked over all the adults and asked, "Dad, who's the big guy here? Is it you or someone else? I just want to know."

Wyndham replied, "Well, I'm in charge of the group, so I guess that means I'm the big guy."

Jacob seemed quite pleased. He smiled and said, "I thought so!"

I often smile when I hear him ask that question or watch him figure it out. Yet, as I think about it, it is a profound question. It is one I asked in making my decision about how I was going to live life and who I wanted to please. I figured that if God was really the master engineer, the ultimate one in charge of creation, the Alpha and the Omega, the "big, big guy," then it should and would radically affect how I live and what I think and who I most want to please. And it is my prayer that Jacob will ultimately figure out who this biggest "big, big guy" is.

As I look around at the way life is often so carelessly lived, I wonder where the fear of God has gone. Humanism is the religion of choice where everything centers on what *I* think and what *I* want. In everyday matters and choices, God is so often left out of the picture. Though in the United States our motto is "In God We Trust," we not only lack trust in God, but we are challenged by others if we try to publicly acknowledge him. In a world where tolerance is preached loudly, it is ironic that holding to convictions about God and his resolute standard is seen to be one of the few intolerable things. Where is the simple trust and awe that the one in charge can do anything and do everything?

I am so inspired by real people in history who held on to this reality—like King David, who as a young boy defied the enemies of God. Against all logic and peer pressure he knew that his God could defeat the giant through his small slingshot because God was and is the ultimate one in charge. This fact gave him great courage, and he did not hesitate to speak his convictions.

How often do we let the "giants" stop us today? Do we let fear of confronting the common beliefs and practices of this world keep us from speaking up and speaking out with confidence? When this happens, we are like the cowardly Israelite soldiers, allowing ourselves to be taunted by unbelievers. We shrink back rather than showing the crowd who our great God really is—the one true God.

The world today tries to tell us how to live and for whom to live; peers are persuading us to pursue certain lifestyles; jobs are calling us to give more and more of our time and our selves. Jacob's question seems an all-important one to ponder...a necessary one to answer. Everything else we do springs from our conviction about the answer to this question, "Who is the big guy here? I mean the big, big guy?"

> Do you not know?
>> Have you not heard?
> Has it not been told you from the beginning?
>> Have you not understood since the earth was founded?
> He sits enthroned above the circle of the earth,
>> and its people are like grasshoppers.
> He stretches out the heavens like a canopy,
>> and spreads them out like a tent to live in.
> He brings princes to naught
>> and reduces the rulers of this world to nothing.
> No sooner are they planted,
>> no sooner are they sown,
>> no sooner do they take root in the ground,
> than he blows on them and they wither,
>> and a whirlwind sweeps them away like chaff.

> "To whom will you compare me?
>> Or who is my equal?" says the Holy One.
> Lift your eyes and look to the heavens:
>> Who created all these?
> He who brings out the starry host one by one,
>> and calls them each by name.
> Because of his great power and mighty strength,
>> not one of them is missing. (Isaiah 40:21-26)

Who Am I?

I myself am convinced, my brothers, that you yourselves are full of goodness, complete in knowledge and competent to instruct one another.

Romans 15:14

Jacob, like other children who were abandoned, sometimes struggles with his identity. Is he Romanian or is he American? Will he go back to live in his home country one day or always live here? Is he really as much a part of the family as everyone else? His skin is bronzed; he has dark hair and brown eyes. When we went to get him in Romania he had dyed his hair blonde to "look more like the family." Jacob goes back and forth between whether he thinks he is black or white. Often when he sees a dark skinned man he gives me his winsome smile and says, "That is my brother."

A few weeks ago Jacob had gotten into trouble at school twice in one week. He thought it would be cool to see what happened if he pushed a friend into the girls' bathroom. He also decided he did not like an activity block to which he was assigned, so he went to another one after being told not to. He was being disrespectful to a teacher he does not like. We had a strong talk with Jacob and took some favorite privileges away from him. I asked him what kind of person he wanted to be, to which he replied, "I think I am both good and evil." I explained that this is a dilemma common to the human race.

I know he has a very different past from his siblings and is unsure how to process this fact. I explained that we all have the potential to be good or evil, and we have to choose our course of life when it comes to right and wrong. We have to make the choice; it is not made for us by another person or by something we cannot control. Though I was not happy with his actions, I reminded Jacob of all the good things in him and who I believe he is and can become.

Though he can look like a tough guy on the outside, inside is someone struggling in his security, identity and feeling of worth. The good thing is that a struggle is going on. He has not given in to feeling insecure and he keeps pushing through. Sometimes his progress is slow, but at other times he grows by leaps and bounds. I want to always help him know how incredibly valuable he is to God, to his family and to so many other people. He is a treasure.

I cannot imagine trying to figure out who I am without God in the picture. Without a spiritual identity, so much of who I am would depend on background, intelligence, culture and race. It is our spiritual identity that truly makes the difference in our security. God sets eternity in the hearts of men (Ecclesiastes 3:11). We are created as spiritual beings. There is no racial or cultural distinction in God's eyes. There is a part of us that will live forever—and that is what God notices. God has always *been* and always will *be*. Jesus knew where he came from and where he was going. My relationship with God is what fills me with deep security and knowledge of who I really am. I need to be reminded of that often. I used to see the Bible as a rulebook given to me to police my life. That was before I came to understand that its purpose is to bring me to a relationship with my Creator and perfect Father.

The world does not give me value. It is out to take and exploit, not to truly care about me. The more I read the Bible, the more I understand that over and over again God is reaching out to me and telling me how much he loves me, and how valuable I am to him. I now see it as a love letter from God. I need his love and am deeply grateful for it.

Though these episodes with Jacob were not pleasant, I see even more clearly how much he needs to know that he is valuable and is "full of goodness." It doesn't excuse the disrespect or disobedience, but the disrespect does not negate what great stuff lies within Jacob.

I decided to begin slipping a note to Jacob often telling him some small thing I love about him. God does that for me in his word, and I know how much I need it and rely on it. It changes me from the inside out.

> For you created my inmost being;
>   you knit me together in my mother's womb.
> I praise you because I am fearfully and wonderfully made;
>   your works are wonderful,
>   I know that full well.
> My frame was not hidden from you
>   when I was made in the secret place.
> When I was woven together in the depths of the earth,
>   your eyes saw my unformed body.
> All the days ordained for me
>   were written in your book
>   before one of them came to be.
>
> How precious to me are your thoughts, O God!
>   How vast is the sum of them! (Psalm 139:13-17)

Keepin' It Simple

> "Not everyone who says to me, 'Lord, Lord,' will enter the kingdom of heaven, but only he who does the will of my Father who is in heaven. Many will say to me on that day, 'Lord, Lord, did we not prophesy in your name, and in your name drive out demons and perform many miracles?' Then I will tell them plainly, 'I never knew you. Away from me, you evildoers!'"
>
> Matthew 7:21-23

I have already told you that Jacob is a "bottom line" kind of person. He is perceptive and quick to figure things out. You won't get much by him. Sometimes I walk into the room when he is watching a movie. I may be putting something away, and he will say, "You're really just wanting to make sure I'm watching something good aren't you? You don't really need to put that away now." I smile. He knows it is because I care, but he figures out a lot of motives behind my actions.

Our family's focus on pleasing God has been somewhat intriguing for Jacob because religion was something someone occasionally came to the orphanage and "did for them." Religion included icons and a bit of ceremony, but not any understanding of personal application to everyday life.

After Jacob had been here about a year, I would notice him commenting about people's love for God or lack thereof. He would hear kids swearing and making suggestive comments or obscene gestures and say, "They don't love God." I did not prompt him, and he wasn't even asking for my opinion. He was just commenting on what was very obvious to him. To Jacob, loving God meant living life very differently from those who do not love God. He perceived that what we said about loving God was carried out in our lifestyles. A very simple concept, but sadly often missed by many of us who have much more sophistication and learning than Jacob.

I remember watching the Academy Awards a little over a year ago. Jacob is very interested in actors, and we were watching the awards ceremony together. After winning an award for a top song for a motion picture, a singing group came to the podium to accept the coveted award. Jacob began laughing and saying, "Yeah right, that is very funny." The group of women were acknowledging their love for God and giving him "the credit" for the award. While I do not know all that was going on in their minds at the time, I know Jacob had something on very straight. He was finding it "a joke" to hear what they were saying. Jacob's connection was again very simple. "Listen to them talk about loving God and look...they have no clothes on."

Sure enough, the clothing (or lack thereof) was so sensual and provocative that we had to change the channel. The words about God became a joke because of what Jacob saw before him. It was simple to him...loving God meant a different way of life, affecting how you talk, what you wear, what you focus on. It wasn't complicated. It was actually quite simple.

Jacob's comments underscore a simple fact: The way we live is a result of our love for God—or lack of love for God. I think about what makes me feel loved. If people do not take the time to know me and if they disregard the things that are important to me, I do not feel loved by them. If on top of that, they were to profess to others and me how much they loved me, I would feel very violated.

Love causes us to live for someone in a way that puts him or her above ourselves. After my first three children were born, my love for them was shown by the way I treated them. Yes, often I would long just to gaze at them, and the warm feelings of motherhood would exude throughout my soul. However, sometimes in the middle of the night when they cried and needed to be changed and fed, the warm, fuzzy feelings would not be present. The commitment to love them was present, and that superceded the feelings. I never debated about getting up and feeding them, though often it went against what I was "feeling."

Often in my marriage I feel incredibly in love and all romantic and tingly. On the other hand, at times I can feel frustrated or angry and not at all romantic and tingly. Love for my husband means I strive to treat him the same no matter what I might currently feel. Leaving him or being unfaithful to him is not an option that I ever entertain because I love him.

I love my husband and my children with all of my heart. It is important to me that they feel loved by me. To do that I have spent many years learning more and more about them, spending time with them, talking to them, trusting them. I try to make them happy because that is what love is all about. The feelings fluctuate in strength, but the decision to love is the constant that determines the way I live for them and around them. It determines how I talk to them and about them. Love means learning to please them and put them above myself. I certainly don't do this perfectly, and sometimes I hurt them. However, none of them would ever question my love for them.

In his word God defines what love for him looks like and acts like. How loved by us does he feel? How good are we at expressing our love and living it out? How often do we put his will above ours or find out new ways to please him? He is, after all, King of kings and Lord of lords (Revelation 17:14). He has loved us first and demonstrated the depth of his love by sacrificing his own Son for our good. How we respond truly depends on our love for him. No amount of liturgy, icons, rules or religious heritage will cause us to live a life for God. It springs from our love for him. As I said earlier, I see reading the Bible much like reading a love letter from God. He does not want a form letter sent back to him after he has poured out his heart. He simply wants our heart, our full love. Christianity is simple. It is all about loving God.

At that time Jesus said, "I praise you, Father, Lord of heaven and earth, because you have hidden these things from the wise and learned, and revealed them to little children." (Matthew 11:25)

'My Decision'

"If anyone chooses to do God's will, he will find out whether my teaching comes from God or whether I speak on my own."
John 7:17

'It's my decision, you know." These are words Jacob says often, but they are rather new to him. I have come to understand that freedom of choice has been a true mark of the change from orphan to son.

When Jacob first came, he was very unfamiliar with choices. Choices had never been a part of his life. He had been the property of the state and was not seen as important enough to be given choices. Jacob was never able to choose what he wanted to eat or wear. In the orphanage there was structure, and there was little opportunity to make choices of how to spend time. His activities were predetermined, and if he had stayed in the orphanage, his choices for occupations would have been few. In Romania, once a child finishes eighth grade he must test in order to go to high school. Very few orphans are even given the opportunity to test, so they simply learn to survive on the streets. Trades of choice are prostitution and stealing.

A familiar phrase coming from Jacob during his first few months with us was, "What I do now?" It was tiring for me to come up with enough ideas, jobs and activities to fill his day. He simply did not know what to do with unstructured time. Gradually, he began to get the hang of it, but choosing is not easy. When Jacob first started earning money, he would spend it on things I knew were not wise. The plastic toys would break easily or the computer games would be too difficult or too dull. Having some money was new, and he made some mistakes on how he spent it. But it was important for us to let him make choices on how he spent it. We would give him advice that he sometimes took and sometimes didn't take. As he learned more discernment, he began to ask for more advice.

Choosing food at a restaurant was something to get used to, and choosing what to wear became something he especially appreciated. He asked advice on what looked good, and he learned how to put things together. His bedroom, which used to be Melissa's and decorated Victorian style with lace and porcelain dolls, was soon covered with posters of karate heroes, dogs and cars (and yes, a head shot of Britney Spears). He began to learn his personal value by his ability to make choices.

The lifestyle of a disciple of Jesus is still very new to Jacob. He often asks about what it means to be a Christian. He has stated at times that he might get baptized when he is fifty, and then he looks to see our response. He wants to know that he will be loved no matter what. We will explain to him the consequences of his choice, but he must ultimately make the choice. Like Jesus with the rich young ruler in Matthew 19 or the father in the story of the prodigal son in Luke 15, I must love him enough to let him choose. His own choice and decision to love God is what will make it lasting. He knows our deepest desire for him. He also knows it is a decision that is a big one, and one he has to be ready to make. All we can do is show him who God is, who Jesus is, the value of the decision to follow him and the consequences of a life without God. I wish I could make that decision for him, but I cannot. I pray always that he will make the right decision as the stakes eternally are huge.

I often think how much easier it would be on the heart of God if he caused us all to choose him. However, that would take away our value of being created in the image of God. Love would not have the same meaning without the opportunity of choice. Choice gives great value to life. Every meaningful thing we do is really based on our ability to choose. Though we might think that our love for God or even a spouse is based on feelings, it is really a decision. That is good news because when we make the choice to live for God, it supercedes feelings and circumstances…though usually feelings will follow.

I am grateful that God's decision to love me wasn't based on feelings and circumstances. He chose to go to the cross because of that love. I know Jesus did not *feel* like sweating drops of blood while praying in the garden before his crucifixion. He even asked for his Father to spare him from such a terrible death and separation. Yet, God gives us a glimpse into his heart in Isaiah 53 when the prophecy of Jesus' crucifixion includes Jesus seeing the "light of life" and being satisfied after the suffering of his soul. The cross was worth it to Jesus because of what it did for us. That is amazing love springing from a decision to love us unconditionally. God chose to love us when we were most unlovable. I love showing Jacob scriptures that talk about the Jacob of the Bible and how God chose him.

I am grateful that by giving Jesus, God chose Jacob and God chose me. I am grateful that Jesus chose to love us, adopt us and give us salvation.

Jacob's phrase, "It's my decision, you know," holds a lot of meaning. It is a phrase we all need to understand and own. The purpose and meaning in my life and where I spend eternity is "my decision, you know."

> "But if serving the Lord seems undesirable to you, then choose for yourselves this day whom you will serve, whether the gods your forefathers served beyond the River, or the gods of the Amorites, in whose land you are living. But as for me and my household, we will serve the Lord." (Joshua 24:15)

The Advocate

In the same way, the Spirit helps us in our weakness. We do not know what we ought to pray for, but the Spirit himself intercedes for us with groans that words cannot express. And he who searches our hearts knows the mind of the Spirit, because the Spirit intercedes for the saints in accordance with God's will.

Romans 8:26-27

'Get out of here, boy! You're here to steal things. You are not welcome. You have no mother!"

The storekeeper at the roadside souvenir shop was speaking to Jacob. My friend Radu through translation gave me a portion of what this woman was saying. I booked it over to her, looked her in the face and said, "I'm his mother!" Now we had not yet adopted Jacob; I could not speak Romanian and she could not speak English. However, she had no trouble understanding what I was saying. I have raised puppies in the past. And as much as I love dogs, I am not fluent in their language. None the less, I have never misunderstood a mother dog's message when she is telling someone to back off from her babies. I think I used this same language. After I spoke to her, Jacob was quite welcome in the shops.

Many times Jacob has needed someone to speak up for him.

"You don't understand! This child will be lost in the big classroom. You've got to take care of him. I love him as if he were my son!" These were the words of Jacob's fifth grade teacher, Tom Ciarlone. He spoke these words as we were gathered with Jacob's team of teachers for the following school year. Most of them really didn't seem to be in tune to Jacob's situation or try to really understand it. Mr. Ciarlone seemed to sense this and felt concern for Jacob's future. His gap in schooling and language was going to make middle school difficult, and Mr. Ciarlone was fighting for Jacob's success.

Everyone needs an advocate.

So, middle school came for Jacob. Imagine your second year in a foreign country with assignments like writing different styles of poetry, a book report a month, studying the feudal system in China and figuring percentages of different types of gases in the atmosphere. In each subject you are given homework that you don't understand, and it takes two hours a night with major help to finish just some of it. As you can imagine, he was lost and getting more and more behind. He felt very unsuccessful but diligently went after his work each night.

I sent letter one, letter two, letter three and begged for help in several teacher conferences that I initiated. I needed someone who could take him where he was and work with him. Nothing changed. My pleas seemed to fall on deaf ears until I got the attention of the right person: one of the school administrators, Ms. Abati. She made things happen quickly—things that others said could not be done. I remember when she first called me. She was amazed that Jacob had not received more help, and after testing we came up with a plan just right for Jacob next year. He will get help beginning with where he is and work at the levels of progress he makes. Tears ran down my face as I talked with her. I was so grateful for her advocacy for my son.

One teacher who never seemed to "get it" told me that Jacob could not remember things and had trouble learning. Yes, he has struggles, but he needs help in overcoming the struggles and finding solutions. About the same time, Jacob's karate *sensei* approached me and shared that he felt Jacob was quite smart because when he told him and showed him something once he had it from then on. One believed in him and one did not.

I appreciate friends like the Pierces, who treat Jacob like their own, and Aunt Mary Ann who goes out of her way to make Jacob feel special. Each of them and many others have helped shape his life, and I am forever grateful. I have never been so aware of the need for an advocate than now with Jacob.

I feel deeply for those who do not have people in their lives advocating for them. I now try to look and listen for those around me who need an advocate—someone to help them be successful. I may not be able to give help to them myself, but I can find it for them. That will only happen, though, if I love them enough. I know it takes persistence and does not end with one try, or even several tries. I deeply appreciate the teachers, Jacob's soccer coach and his karate teacher who in various ways believe in him. I find that he, like all of us, rises to what people believe he can be and do.

I feel more keenly than ever the need to be an advocate, and more appreciative than ever for what it means to have one. I am also more aware and appreciative of my need for an advocate before God, and what Jesus and the Spirit of God do for me over and over, day by day. It gives me such great confidence to know that God's Spirit intercedes for me in my prayers and to know that Jesus is mediating on my behalf before God. Without that, I will be defeated. With my advocate, I am more than a conqueror.

For there is one God and one mediator between God and men, the man Christ Jesus, who gave himself as a ransom for all men. (1 Timothy 2:5-6a)

The Road Race

Therefore, since we are surrounded by such a great cloud of witnesses, let us throw off everything that hinders and the sin that so easily entangles, and let us run with perseverance the race marked out for us. Let us fix our eyes on Jesus, the author and perfecter of our faith, who for the joy set before him endured the cross, scorning its shame, and sat down at the right hand of the throne of God. Consider him who endured such opposition from sinful men, so that you will not grow weary and lose heart.

Hebrews 12:1-3

Jacob and I watched and cheered as the children crossed the finish line. We were back in Romania and the children of the HOPE *worldwide* Family Center were participating in a 1K road race. The temperature on this summer afternoon was 110 degrees Fahrenheit, and these amazing kids were running with all of their might. I love these kids, and they are very special to Jacob as well. I have had the incredible privilege of knowing them for the past several months. Each one of them has a special story and is on an amazing journey. I am grateful for the Family Center and the love and care it provides for these children. My main prayer, however, is that they can begin new journeys with families who adopt them.

As Ionela, Claudia and Alex crossed the finish line, my eyes filled with tears. These siblings had come to the home a few days before it opened. They are fifteen, fourteen and twelve years old respectively. Having seen their father walk out on them at a young age, they lived with their mom and her boyfriend. He was so physically abusive that they slept with a bundle of clothes by the bed. When they heard him come in drunk, they would get dressed as warmly as they could, climb out the window and sleep in the field—even on cold winter nights. This to them was better than the beatings.

Four months earlier, the boyfriend had given their mom the ultimatum of him or the children; Mom told the children to get out for good. A neighbor offered them a shed, with one bed, no plumbing and an open furnace. Ionela and Claudia cared for their brother, while Ionela found a way to travel an hour to school each day where she excelled. I watched these gorgeous, bright children cross the finish line while tears filled my eyes. I am so grateful for the love they are receiving, yet I often hear them pray for a family.

My eyes welled up with tears again as Mariana stumbled before she reached the finish and crawled the rest of the way to the tape. She was able to finish because of the cheering and encouragement from the crowd. This child's journey is heroic as well. You see, Mariana is twelve and she is a dwarf. Her little legs are weak, but that did not stop her from running. She is one of Jacob's lifelong friends who grew up with him in the orphanage. I again am thankful for the Family Center where she is loved and nurtured. Yet my heart still rips in two when I leave Romania and she says, "Jeanie, can I come to America and have a family like Jacob has?"

The amazing thing about these children is that they are grateful and happy. They have made a choice to run their journey without bitterness.

As I write now (on an airplane again) I reflect on a woman I had the honor of being with last evening in Berlin, Germany. She was formerly Miss Colorado and a Dallas Cowboys' cheerleader. She lives in Berlin now where she became a disciple. She also is engaged to a wonderful Christian musician. Recently, she developed a malignant brain tumor that is now a "level four." Though very young, she is in the winter of her journey. She is to be married soon. Last night she performed at a conference, which was one of her last wishes. As she sang an original composition she was accompanied on the piano by her fiancé. She wore a wig to cover her now bald head as she sang the song entitled, "Lucky Every Day." She sang her belief that she is one of the luckiest people alive because she knows God, is part of his family and is going to heaven.

Every person on earth is running a race on his or her journey through life. We often feel like Mariana, stumbling toward the finish line while we watch others seemingly cruise by us. Mariana stumbled over and over again, but she crossed the finish line.

Or we can be the ones who cruise by, but fail to help out the *Marianas* who need help along the way.

What is your attitude about your journey? Do you get bitter or are you "lucky every day"? Are you determined to live for God each day until you cross your finish line? How well do you encourage and help other people cross their finish lines? Some of them need a family; some of them need your encouragement. But they all need your involvement.

I have fought the good fight, I have finished the race, I have kept the faith. (2 Timothy 4:7)

'I Used to Be That Kid'

I know your deeds, your hard work and your perseverance. I know that you cannot tolerate wicked men, that you have tested those who claim to be apostles but are not, and have found them false. You have persevered and have endured hardships for my name, and have not grown weary.

Yet I hold this against you: You have forsaken your first love. Remember the height from which you have fallen! Repent and do the things you did at first.

Revelation 2:2-5a

Enough was enough. The kid's pocket was already full of change. This little beggar had become Jacob's shadow, continually holding out his hand and wanting more money. Jacob kept going back into his pocket and dishing out more for the boy. We were visiting in Romania, and our group was targeted by a deluge of sweaty, dirty palms opened in anticipation of being filled with money. I felt happy doing my duty, giving out a few coins and buying several ice cream cones that brought big smiles from the recipients. However, things were getting a little annoying, as the little guys, tattered and dirty, were so persistent. I thought I had better share a few words of wisdom with Jacob, as he was being accosted time after time with repeaters who had already gotten their prize. I could see clearly that Jacob was not using discretion in his generosity since he gave to the same one numerous times and was even giving away some of his own possessions. This of course was not wise, as they would just need to be replaced. So I explained to Jacob the tactics of the children and his need to just say no. Otherwise, they would never leave him alone.

Jacob looked at me face to face and said, "Mom, when I was little I used to be that kid, only I had to come out in my underwear. I really liked it when somebody gave to me. So it's like this—this is mine and as long as I have it, I'll give it. Why should I stop now?"

I felt as though a knife had been thrust into my heart. I replied to Jacob, "That's a good thought son; why don't you just keep on giving."

When did my heart start to get hard? I started pondering this question. When I first encountered these street children years ago, I was deeply disturbed and cried many tears over them. My heart ached as I prayed for them and thought of ways to help. Since then, I have done a lot of good things. In fact, there I was in Romania with a group of teenagers doing service for the poor. I had been instrumental in opening a home for orphans there, and I even adopted a child. However, it seems that over the course of time I got so busy in my job of helping people and doing good things that I started crying fewer tears. I had gotten used to seeing people who were hurting. Jacob's words stung in my ears as he reminded me that he "used to be that kid" who kept on. I realized that except by the grace of God I, too, was that kid.

This incident helps me think of how God must feel as we go about our days "doing" without "connecting" with the recipients of our gifts, or with the one who is the source of all we have to give. I realized that when this happens, it is very easy to get annoyed with the pressing and persistent needs that surround us and to become more humanistic than spiritual in our thinking. I was cut deeply as I thought about the words of Paul in 1 Corinthians 13:3: "If I give all I possess to the poor and surrender my body to the flames, but have not love, I gain nothing."

I thought about God's warnings of relying on past righteousness (good deeds we often think we can store up) in

Ezekiel 18:24-32 and of losing our first love. I want to see others and their needs the way Jacob saw the kids who were begging. To do this I know I must train my heart and mind to think of what is going on in their lives day by day. I must truly see people as through the eyes of Jesus.

I pray to see each new day as an opportunity and responsibility to imitate Jesus in the way he gave to others until his last breath. He stayed connected to them and connected to God. He is such an upward call to me. I pray that you and I will, like Jacob, remember where we have come from and each day ask the question "Why should I stop now?"

> Let us not become weary in doing good, for at the proper time we will reap a harvest if we do not give up. Therefore, as we have opportunity, let us do good to all people, especially to those who belong to the family of believers. (Galatians 6:9-10)

Ready and Waiting

34

> *"O Jerusalem, Jerusalem, you who kill the prophets and stone those sent to you, how often I have longed to gather your children together, as a hen gathers her chicks under her wings, but you were not willing."*
>
> Matthew 23:37

Thanksgiving Day wasn't supposed to be like this. It had been a good morning sitting in the bleachers for the annual Burlington High School Thanksgiving Day football game. This was Sam's last game of the season and his football career, and the whole family was there to watch him play as the team closed out an incredible season. We were in layers of clothing and covered with down comforters as we sat in near zero temperatures. We all cheered as Sam played a good game and, along with his team members, celebrated the victory.

At home the hot cider, sausage balls, shrimp cocktail and chicken salad awaited us. I still needed to complete the preparation of the turkey, cornbread stuffing, homemade rolls and mashed potatoes. We all hurried to the car, eager for welcomed warmth.

Jacob had gone to the car earlier, which was okay as it was so cold outside. He had taken the key so he could listen to music and get some heat. That was okay too because he had proven to be trustworthy. But when we got back to the car, it was in a different parking place. Jacob is fourteen, with no license and has only practiced driving a very few times in a parking lot with his dad. He had moved the car down the street. We were not happy, to say the least. We tried to explain that doing this was unsafe and illegal. His only response was to try and prove that he was a perfect driver, knew everything about it and would never need lessons. He went on to talk about how he knew how to do everything and needed no help

120

or lessons on anything. I was amazed at his stubbornness. He did not need to learn from anyone—he had things all figured out. Jacob had not wanted to be at the game, and he didn't like anything about the day. He was not happy and was spreading his negativity.

Later, as we sat down at the table to thank God for the day and our Thanksgiving feast, we had to send him to his room because of his poor attitude. He left us no choice. I knew it was the right thing to do, but my heart ached. It was really sad to see that empty place at the table. I longed for him to change his attitude and join us, eat with us and laugh with us. He just would not change it.

After about an hour, his Aunt Mary Ann (who he was not on the "outs" with) went to his room and had a talk with him. They have a special friendship. The talk helped, his attitude improved and he joined us. Things were better, but we did not have relational resolution between us. I do not do well without resolution. I have to have closure and cannot just continue on and pretend nothing happened. Though I was happy for this improvement, things were awkward.

Thanksgiving is my favorite holiday. The family had a wonderful time together in front of a roaring fire, and later in the evening we went out to a movie. There were no further incidents with Jacob, but I knew relationally that it still did not feel good. He had not been humble, so we were not resolved. It was late, and he went on to bed.

I walked into his room a bit later, hurting from the distance between us and was praying as he slept. I was praying for his heart to be soft. After a few moments he stuck his head up and asked, "You watching me sleep?"

"Yeah, sort of," I answered. "I was actually hoping you had something to say to me."

"I'm sorry, Mom."

"I forgive you, Jacob. I love you. Good night."

I kissed him and walked out the door, thankful that things were back to normal and it had been a good Thanksgiving Day after all.

It seemed ridiculous for Jacob to be so stubborn and prideful. He missed out on a great meal by being unwilling to change his attitude and get humble. I'm sure there are difficult things that family holidays bring out for him, but he still has to get humble and grateful. I know the pain I felt from being unresolved with Jacob is only a fraction of what God feels toward me when I am being stubborn and prideful. I am sure God must shake his head, wondering why I just won't "humble out" and enjoy the feast. It sure is easy to see the need to get humble when I am not the one being challenged.

I am amazed by the constancy of Jesus' love as he watched over the stubborn, prideful hearts of his people. I'm sure I would have been tempted to zap them all for their arrogance. However, Jesus wept over them and longed to gather them as a mother hen gathers her chicks. I am grateful, for I realize I am deserving of the zap!

When I was watching Jacob sleep, I thought about how much God desires perfect resolution with me. He is so ready to forgive. He is just waiting for me to get humble. And when I do, an amazing thing happens. He completely forgives.

I like to think that when I go to God with a humble, soft heart he says, "I forgive you. I love you." And he gives me a kiss.

For as high as the heavens are above the earth,
  so great is his love for those who fear him;
as far as the east is from the west,
  so far has he removed our transgressions from us.
As a father has compassion on his children,
  so the LORD has compassion on those who fear him;
for he knows how we are formed,
  he remembers that we are dust. (Psalm 103:11-14)

The Judge

35

"For God did not send his Son into the world to condemn the world, but to save the world through him. Whoever believes in him is not condemned, but whoever does not believe stands condemned already because he has not believed in the name of God's one and only Son. This is the verdict: Light has come into the world, but men loved darkness instead of light because their deeds were evil. Everyone who does evil hates the light, and will not come into the light for fear that his deeds will be exposed. But whoever lives by the truth comes into the light, so that it may be seen plainly that what he has done has been done through God."

John 3:17-21

We arrived early as we did not know quite what to expect. We searched eagerly for the face of our lawyer. A line was forming outside of the closed doors. Teenage boys were dressed in suits. Men and women with briefcases were looking over notes. I overheard a woman talking about her divorce case and listened as boys talked with their parole officers. The doors opened and everyone scurried in.

Even though Jacob had been legally adopted in Romania, we had been advised to have him adopted in America as well. So here we were in the courtroom. I stuck close to our lawyer, along with Wyndham and Jacob, and we found a seat near the back of the ominous-looking, packed room. Our lawyer said we might be there for hours. He hoped the judge would hear our case early, but we did not know. There was nervous talking in the room until someone came and asked everyone to be quiet. An aura of fear and awe pervaded the room.

All of a sudden everyone in the room stood up. The judge walked into the room to complete silence. Though we knew we were there for a happy reason, I still felt butterflies in my stomach.

123

The judge asked everyone to be seated. Imagine my surprise when I heard the next words out of his mouth: "Would everyone clear the courtroom except for the Shaw case!"

Was I hearing correctly? Everyone clear the courtroom? My heart was pounding. What was happening?

As quickly as everyone had come in, everyone cleared out. Some people sneered, as they felt a bit inconvenienced. Why was he clearing the courtroom? Wyndham, Jacob, our lawyer and I moved up to the front and stood before the judge at his request. Jacob was not quite sure what was going on. Neither were we.

The judged looked at Jacob and looked at us and smiled. He asked Jacob, "Do you want to be part of this family?" Jacob replied with affirmation, and then the judge had another question for him.

"Jacob Richard Shaw, what is your favorite restaurant here in America?" By this time Jacob was grinning and said, "I think it is '99'." (Jacob likes the club sandwiches and ribs.) The judge started writing and tore off a slip of paper.

"You are ordered by the court to celebrate this joyous occasion of your American adoption with your parents and siblings at 99 Restaurant before sundown three days from now. Now, get your camera out and let's commemorate this great occasion."

He put his arms around us and had the bailiff take a picture of him with the happy family. He explained to us that he cleared the courtroom because he wanted to enjoy this special time and begin his day with great news, as all the other cases he would be hearing were not good news.

Later that evening, as we sat around the table at the 99 Restaurant with our entire family, we shared with all the kids the story of the judge. We had already developed the picture from the day, and everyone was amazed at the judge's interaction with us. There was much chatter around the table as congratulatory remarks to Jacob could be heard all around. We ordered our meals and felt compelled to share with the waitress and anyone who would listen to our good news of the day. We were eager to brag about the judge and his handling of the case. Though it was very sobering, we were there not for judgment but for adoption.

My eyes welled up with tears as I realized how analogous this day was to a day we will have sometime in the future. We will stand before the great Judge and have him put his arms around us, celebrating with us the good news of our heavenly adoption.

> For I am already being poured out like a drink offering, and the time has come for my departure. I have fought the good fight, I have finished the race, I have kept the faith. Now there is in store for me the crown of righteousness, which the Lord, the righteous Judge, will award to me on that day—and not only to me, but also to all who have longed for his appearing. (2 Timothy 4:6-8)

Citizenship

Consequently, you are no longer foreigners and aliens, but fellow citizens with God's people and members of God's household, built on the foundation of the apostles and prophets, with Christ Jesus himself as the chief cornerstone. In him the whole building is joined together and rises to become a holy temple in the Lord. And in him you too are being built together to become a dwelling in which God lives by his Spirit.
Ephesians 2:19-22

Jacob has a red passport. At present, he is a Romanian citizen with a permanent resident card. Jacob can travel with us back and forth from the United States. He can attend public school and even in a few years get a job. But he is not satisfied.

"When will I be an American citizen, Mom?" Jacob asks.

I have explained to Jacob that we have applied for his citizenship. He first had his American adoption where his name became Jacob Richard Shaw, instead of Iacob. His birth date is September 14, 1986. We then filled out all the necessary paperwork and took it in person to the immigration office in Boston. I was so surprised when they told me to expect his oath of citizenship to be about thirty-four months from then. Perhaps it will be sooner. I hope so. Jacob feels that something is missing. He would like to have that blue passport and be able to say that he, like the rest of his family, is an American.

When we celebrated Independence Day last year, we explained to Jacob more of the history behind it. After he saw the movie *The Patriot*, he understood even more. I feel honored to be a citizen of the United States of America and to experience all the freedom that comes with it, and I long to share that gift with him.

Jacob waits for his citizenship. We plan to celebrate on that day. He won't be just waiting for citizenship, or be "kind of" a citizen. He will be a full citizen, with all the rights and responsibilities attached to that privilege.

When I stand in passport lines to enter different countries, I notice that some individuals must stay in line a very long time. Sometimes they are asked many questions. They hold passports from many different nations. Seldom have I had to wait or be questioned because of the respect shown to citizens of the United States. There is something wonderful about that blue passport. It brings with it so many privileges. Even with its own set of problems, citizenship in America is a privilege. I can vote for my government, I can receive all the public and social services the country offers.

Citizenship in heaven, however, is "blow away." There are no problems in heaven. There will be no death, no tears and no poverty. There will be no regrets in heaven—only perfect peace and happiness. It is beyond my comprehension. The apostle John tells us that heaven is wonderful beyond any words he could speak. I realize I don't think about it enough. Focusing on heaven puts a lot of things in perspective, especially time. I am a resident of earth, but I am a citizen of heaven. I long to share that gift with others.

Think about it.

I hope one day to see you there.

But our citizenship is in heaven. And we eagerly await a Savior from there, the Lord Jesus Christ, who, by the power that enables him to bring everything under his control, will transform our lowly bodies so that they will be like his glorious body. (Philippians 3:20-21)

Note: Jacob has now received both his American citizenship and his blue passport!

When It Happened

In Reflection

I'm not quite sure when it happened...whether it was the first time I saw him with his brown curly hair, his skinny frame, his dirty hands and torn up shoes...and he flashed that big ol' smile...

or maybe it was the years of anticipation and disappointments of waiting and waiting...

or when I saw the fear in his eyes when he left his "home" and then ran away to prolong his departure. Maybe it was his willingness to leave everything he had known and to try to just survive...or the realization that I was privileged enough to learn unconditional love when he was not happy or easy those first weeks.

It must have been watching him on his first picnic eat four hamburgers and two hot dogs as if he would never see food again...and later learning that he had hunted for food in trash cans.

Surely, it was him catching his first fish, hoping to catch more and bigger fish than his dad...then showing me the picture of his fish and saying, "Fish crying...water his house."

Maybe it was at the carnival after three weeks in America where he won his goldfish—he thought it was to eat. When it died, he looked at me and said, "Fish, cheemetary?" (cemetery).

Maybe it was his many after-school conversations in Romanian with Jordan his dog...or the look in his eyes when he learned to ride his bike and rode till dark and his hands were bleeding.

Then again, was it his first movie, *Waterboy*? It was difficult to decide which was funnier…the movie or him doubled over with belly laughter…

or his prayers at night that include so many people and soon went from Romanian to English…

or the wrestling with his brother or the "Oh Gosh" and rolling his eyes…joyfully enduring the many hugs, kisses and "You're so cute" from his sister…

or his asking, "What's so cute? You like my hair, my eyes?…Tell me."

Maybe it was when he received his school pictures and was so excited that he taped them to the window facing out so I'd see them when I drove up…

or was it after school when he said, "I missed you," giving me a giant hug that he said would last "for one hour," though after about a minute he let go, laughed and said, "I don't think so."

Surely it was when he put his hands on his hips, looked me in the eyes and said, "I'm cereal," and then sat down to eat his "serious and milk."

Was it the gleam in his eye when he was able to help, or when he earned some money and then went with me to the grocery and spent it all on flowers for me and his two sisters…and of course didn't let me bring any of the groceries in, insisting that he would bring them all in?

Maybe it was his writing his "grandmother" and slipping money he had earned into the envelope…

or looking for Melissa's missing book in the "chicken" by the "fridgidairy."

Perhaps it was the joy of watching him meet his grandparents, aunts, uncles and cousins and the respect he showed his family…

or that first Christmas morning after all the kids had slept on the floor of Melissa's room on Christmas eve, or watching him at the top of the stairs jumping up and down in anticipation, or the exuberance over his gifts...

or watching his beaming smile as he, in his tuxedo, walked me down the aisle at his sister's wedding.

Or maybe it was the day when we were walking downtown and he took my hand and said, "Never before did I walk with my mom...I mean never when I was a baby did I walk with my mom."

I'm really not quite sure just when and where it happened.

All I know is that somewhere along the way, our hearts became entwined and began to beat as one—I became his mother and he became my son.

Jeanie Shaw
July 1999

EPILOGUE

As of March 1999, there were 547,000 children in foster care in the United States (AFCARS 2000). The United States Department of Health and Human Services estimates that as many as 117,000 children currently in foster care need adoptive families. Worldwide, the statistics are even more sobering:

- There are an estimated 150 million children who call the streets of the world home. (UNICEF, 1998) Many of these children are abandoned.
- Mexico City has 1,900,000 kids on the streets, 240,000 of them are abandoned. (Action International, 1996)
- Brazil may have the most abandoned children in the world; their numbers range from 12 to 24 million. (Relin, 1991)
- 62% of the girls on Brazilian streets will either commit suicide or be murdered before they are 18. (Switz.)
- 800,000 girls 12-16 years old are prostitutes in Thailand. Parents sell children into bondage. (UNICEF, 1991)
- An estimated 260,000 children went to institutions in Romania as a result of Ceausescu's dictatorship.
- There are approximately 1,000,000 orphans in South Africa due to AIDS. It is a growing epidemic. (Children's Ministries Convention, 1996)

These numbers and statistics represent precious individuals with a past, present and future of some kind. Each of these children is on a journey.

One of the greatest privileges in my life has been to visit with some of these children who are referred to as statistics. Some live on trash heaps in the Philippines, some in tin shacks in Mexico. I have played with orphaned children who are battling AIDS in South Africa. Others huddle around an

open fire in India by night and beg throughout the day. I have
visited children (and their children) in the sewers of Romania
and spent hours with others in institutions. I have had the
opportunity to hear from children living in group homes in
my own sophisticated city of Boston, and to hear children
currently in foster care tell their heart-wrenching stories.

Most of the children I talk to do not know what "family"
really means, but they know they want a family. We were created by God to be in a family, and they know it. I suppose I
will never quit shedding tears as I talk to these children.
However, I have encountered some bright spots along the path
of some children's journeys. Here are a few of their stories:

Abbey was taken into foster care as an infant. She was
born addicted to heroin and nearly died. A loving family took
her in and transformed this anxious, unhappy baby into a
healthy, happy little girl. A few months ago she was adopted
into this family and joyfully squealed, "I adopted, I adopted."

Two siblings became part of a wonderful family (soon to be
adopted) and are learning to trust and be secure. Prior to this,
one of these boys had witnessed his father murder his mother.

This week was Annie's adoption. She entered a family who
already had four children. She came into the family having
been severely neglected, living in a house where she witnessed
much drug use and sexual activity. Annie came in hitting, kick-
ing, biting, screaming and swearing at everyone in sight. She
did not know how to give or receive love—and now she is an
amazingly loving and outgoing little girl.

Yesterday I watched a video of a close friend's visit to
Romania. There he told the three Lupu children (Ionela,
Claudia and Alex—see chapter 32) that he, his wife and their
three children wanted to ask them to be a part of their family.
Tears rolled down my cheeks as Jacob and I watched this
video and we saw the children sob with joy and hold on to
their new father like they never wanted to let go. They should
be adopted by their new family before the year is over.

Harold is currently serving as a church administrator. He grew up in several foster care situations and was even sent out of one because he was so angry and out of control. He was told that he would never amount to anything and he believed it, doing terrible in school. A family and teacher who decided to love Harold on his journey turned his life around and convinced him of the truth: he was very bright and had so much going for him. He is married and a wonderful man, contributing so much to those around him.

Jesse is currently on the full-time ministry staff. He was adopted from an orphanage when he was five years old. He now has a wonderful family of his own, and as a minister he helps many others along their journey.

A year and a half ago I helped welcome seventeen orphans into our Family Center in Romania (see chapter 4). As I left the country the following week, I wondered if we had made a big mistake, but counted on the power of God and the power of his love. The children were out of control, screaming, rocking wildly and trying to jump out of windows. I stand in awe of God when I go back now and talk, sing, play and pray with happy, controlled children who love life and are so grateful to God for the love they receive daily. The difference in these children in just this short time is staggering. When I walk in now, it feels like home...and it feels like family. However, the children still want a family of their own that will last forever. The children always ask me when I leave, "Jeanie, can you find me a home like Jacob has? I want to have a family." They pray at night for a family.

When we started this home, I asked Jacob what would be different for the children. He responded by telling me that every single thing about life would be different. You could not even compare how much better it would be for the children.

I asked Jacob if he would like to contribute to this book and here is what he wrote:

When my mom asked me what I thought about her writing a book about me, I thought it would be really cool. I think it will be nice to have when I am an adult, so I can remember what things were like. I don't really like to talk about things back then. I really never thought about what it would mean to be in a family, because I had no idea what a family was. If you don't know what it is, you don't think about it that much. There were fun times but really hard times and bad things. I was hungry a lot. I would feel saddest when parents of the kids in the orphanage came to visit and bring them things. I knew no one would come for me. The scariest times were when a worker would beat me. I remember once when I got beat with a stick with hard things on the end. My skin was all swollen and messed up. I thought about that when I saw a video with Jesus getting beaten. It seemed like that.

My mom asked me if I ever dreamed of having parents. I had a small hope, but it wasn't until I met my mom that I had a dream. I could tell she loved me and I wanted her to be my mom. When I was told I would be adopted, I was happy and a little scared. I was going to have to be different than I was and learn to love parents.

Without a family there is no food and definitely no love. Everything is different. It's good to have a family. I think all the kids need a family. The things that make me know I am part of a family is that I feel loved. I live with them every day and have a place to come home to. A family's love is good. They tell you every day they love you. They encourage you and do stuff for you. They spend time with you and say good night to you. I never had that before.

I am so privileged to walk beside Jacob on his journey. Not every child has a victory story—but many have and soon there will be more victories! The need is so great. Our response to the need will determine the future for these children.

Each time we drive through the perimeter of Bucharest we are likely to see groups of girls soliciting prostitution. Eighty-five percent of orphans here end up this way, or as drug addicts, alcoholics or victims of suicide. I cry for these children, and yet I know that with help *one at a time* they can have hope and a future. I am reminded of a favorite anecdote:

A man and his wife were walking on a beach. As far as they could see, thousands of starfish were stranded on the beach and dying. The wife bent down, picked up a starfish and threw it back into the sea.

Her husband asked, "What are you doing?"

She said, "I'm throwing it back into the sea."

He replied, "Why bother? This beach is miles long and you can't possibly make a difference."

The woman knelt, picked up another starfish and threw it back into the sea.

"I just made a difference," she said, "to that one."

I am challenged to ask myself how long and far will I go to see another child, another soul find hope and a future? Will I let myself be paralyzed by thinking I am so insignificant that I can't make a difference in this world? That is the kind of thinking that leaves God out of the picture. I must do what I can do, and God, with his perfect timing and power, will oversee and orchestrate it all.

What will you do?

Dad and Jacob after a successful fishing trip

The Call to Adopt

Wyndham Shaw

My work as a Vice President of Hope *worldwide* has given me the opportunity to travel to many of the most needy places in the world. From India to China and South America to Romania, there are millions of orphans in deep distress because of abandonment and lack of love. One of my goals for life is to champion the cause of adoption and the practice of true religion.

The Need

An estimated thirty million abandoned children live with the wound of being unwanted or at least of not knowing of the love their birth parents have for them. Psalm 68:6 says, "God sets the lonely in families." His heart and his plan is to provide for them emotionally, physically and spiritually. Disciples are the salt of the earth and the light of the world, taught by God to love deeply and from the heart just as he has loved us. When viewed as a whole, the statistic of thirty million orphans sounds overwhelming. But if each of us determines to make a difference one by one—how, where and with whom we can—God's plan for lonely children will be fulfilled.

In China baby girls were once drowned in rivers. Now more than one million are in orphanages and are in need of homes. In India babies are dropped off in cradles that have been set at the doors of orphanages to help prevent mothers from doing away with the babies. More than thirteen million children are in need of homes in that country alone. In Romania more than 150,000 children live in state-run institutions—in a country with a total population of only twenty-three million. Hundreds of thousands of orphans in Cambodia, Russia and Bulgaria—

and many other nations in Africa, Latin America and around the world—are distressed and lonely, awaiting God's hand to move on their behalf. Like the lost, these children wait to become the objects of disciples' compassion, benevolence and labors of love.

Jesus championed the cause and innocence of children when he took them in his arms to bless them. He rebuked his disciples for not making time or giving attention to them. Disciples today must not be guilty of the same neglect and disdain for the children whom Jesus wants to bless. We must let the little children come to us, our homes, our tables, our extra bedrooms and our arms as we become champions of the fatherless, following Jesus in heart and action! Some would say adoption is not for everyone, and I would agree, but it is for many more than have presently accepted God's call in James 1:27:

> Religion that God our Father accepts as pure and faultless is this: to look after orphans and widows in their distress and to keep oneself from being polluted by the world.

True religion is the command of God for all disciples.

There are currently more orphans in distress in the world than at any time in history. We all are responsible before God to take care of orphans and widows in their distress. While traveling throughout the world, I have seen babies lying in their urine and excrement. Children around the world and in our own cities and towns are dying daily of starvation, both physical and emotional. Whether we take them in, contribute money for their care or become big brothers and sisters to those being cared for by others, we cannot obey Scripture or be like Jesus if we do not take care of them in some way.

I am committed to championing orphans by my example, message and ongoing efforts. I applaud the Gempels and many of my fellow geographic HOPE leaders who lead the way in caring for abandoned children through our benevolent programs worldwide. I also commend the hundreds of disciples who have stepped forward to adopt, such as world sector leaders Doug and Joyce Arthur, Scott and Lynne Green, and Marty and Chris Fuqua; kingdom teachers and their wives, such as Douglas and Vicki Jacoby; evangelists and their wives, such as Mark and Nadine Templer; and hundreds of disciples in churches around the world. I want to challenge many more to step forward this year and in the years to come. Young families need to plan for adopting from the beginning of their marriages. Biological and adoptive blends should become a "norm" among us as we fulfill God's will for orphans.

I also want to commend many single women, such as Joan Lapointe, Katie Scott, Peggy Wells and Donna Bracken, who have pioneered single adoptions and fostering, and have found mutual blessings with their children. Single motherhood by choice is a great way to direct the love of our singles to objects of their affection who desperately need what can be so graciously supplied.

Other commendable means of caring for the fatherless that need to be imitated are church adoption funds like the one begun years ago by Randy and Kay McKean in Boston. Randy originated the idea and presented it to the church. Now disciples give more than $100,000 each year to enable disciples to adopt and care for children. More than twenty churches now collect some sort of adoption contribution, but many more need to imitate this example. When leaders lead with such effort, the people willingly offer themselves, and we can all praise the Lord!

The Impact

Tears rolled down my cheeks as I sat in the humble living room of Maria, the elderly lady who lives next door to the orphanage Jacob was in. (See chapter 7 to meet Maria.) She was telling me how it was through the ten years that she watched the way Jacob and the other children in the orphanage were treated. They grew up in a state institution under the Ceausescu regime and immediately after the fall of communism in Eastern Europe. She told of how the children would climb the fence as she walked home and reach out their skinny, anemic arms to beg for food. She told of hearing their screams as drunken workers beat them on a whim of anger or frustration. She told of hearing it so loudly one night that she got out of bed and went to the orphanage to ask what they were doing. She was told to go away, but insisted on entering. She stayed until the screaming subsided. She told of befriending Jacob and inviting him over for freshly baked bread and cookies several days a week and of how he would ask if he could bring others to feel and taste her kindness. She told of how Jacob would make sure each new arrival was always grateful and polite, not wanting to risk the loss of the oasis she provided in a physical and emotional desert. Jacob to this day saves money to give to Maria each year when we return to Romania for the HOPE Youth Corps. He calls her several times a month, never forgetting the relief and care she offered in the darkest hours of his existence.

Maria is a small prototype of what adoptive families, HOPE *worldwide* programs for abandoned children, and disciples practicing James 1:27 can do. The impact of Jesus' touch and blessing through our arms of love and care is both immediate and eternal. Jeanie has effectively recorded in this book many of the ways a family both impacts and is impacted by following Jesus' command to care for orphans. Every family who has adopted can share stories of similar emotion, learning and satisfaction from what happens when we carry out this portion of God's good, perfect and acceptable will.

This appendix expresses the emotional impact that I personally have realized and the memories that this exercise brings up in me. Julia Hannon, Permanent Families Director for HOPE *worldwide* New England, always says that fostering or adoption has an equally positive impact on both the child and the parents. I believe this is true from both personal and observed experience. It teaches unconditional love, selflessness, patience and appreciation for what being family takes and means to all involved. I have gained fresh gratitude for simple things we enjoy in America, the kingdom and my family just by watching Jacob experience and discover these blessings on a daily basis. Through him I have discovered them again myself. It is like a reconversion of sorts. Through our HOPE *worldwide* Family Center in Saftica, Romania, I have seen what disciples can create by building a family of love, discipline and spirituality out of seventeen abandoned children brought together by God and his disciples under one roof. Jim and Sarah Bolton, disciples from Springfield, Massachusetts, are doing a heroic job forging a family from a Romanian staff committed to practicing pure religion with these abandoned children. In less than a year the children have gone from being out of control, disrespectful, rebellious and generally dysfunctional to being a true family, expressing affection, self-control, respect and joy with each other.

In November 2000, Jeanie and I had the great joy of assisting in the baptism of Ionela, the oldest girl (sixteen years old) in the home. Randy and Kay McKean, Bob and Pat Gempel, Val and Irene Koha and Bob Tranchell (who oversees our churches in the Balkan States) were able to be there for this crying good time as God adopted for his own one of these abandoned children. Ionela is the first of many such stories of the fatherless being united with their heavenly father. Many more are yet to come as we practice true religion more and more!

The Cost

What does it take to adopt a child, staff an orphanage or run a foster care agency? More than anything, it takes faith, hope and love. It takes faith to believe in something and act on that belief when you cannot see the outcome before you do it. Adopting is scary because you are taking others' biological products and making yourself responsible for what they become. I believe this takes more faith than conceiving our own children whom we know from the womb and who share our blood and genes. Love in adoption is by necessity more of the *agape* or unconditional variety because there is no natural connection drawing us. Adoptive children and foster children do not look, smell or act like you in the way that biological children tend to. Your love is by choice and commitment, and from that comes affection and attraction. It is the same for the child. Jacob at first did not know what to make of our offering and attempts at love and affection. It was foreign to him and strange. He often would ask, "Why you give me a kiss or a hug?" The great thing is that the longer he has felt it and tried it, the more he likes, relies on and even initiates it. Hope is the ability to persevere because you believe in the eventual positive outcome. Pat Gempel is aptly and affectionately known as "Mama HOPE" by those of us who work with her. She exudes the confidence like few others that we can and will make a difference if we but try and give God room to work.

Hope also springs from the support of those who endure with you through the dark and difficult times of working with orphans who do not always respond quickly or with appreciation to the commitment we make to them. I am no longer naïve about the pain, suffering and plain hard work it takes to care for orphans in their distress. The distress from which they come has not been without effect. They have been wounded and need healing. They have been abandoned and fear it happening again. Parents who take them in must be prepared for the physical, financial, emotional and spiritual challenges they will require. The cross is the ultimate symbol of God's love, not because love is easy, but because it is costly. My challenge would be, for those who hit the painful times of tough love that adoption requires, to not shrink back. Nor should we question why we should take on such a sacrifice. Rather, let us share in the sufferings of Jesus joyfully and with the heart to learn obedience through the things we suffer here as well as in all other aspects of following our Lord!

Equally as important as the heart of sacrifice of those who adopt is the commitment of those who support them, providing not only financial help but whatever else is needed. In

Boston we are preparing to launch a post-placement program to supplement our foster care services through HOPE *worldwide* New England. The goal of this service will be to provide excellent resources unique to adoptive children that are easily available to our families who have taken in children. The services will include a resource library, art therapy for children, support groups for parents, and seminars to bring in experts in the adoption field to address challenges unique to adoptive families and to provide solutions. Bottom line, anything of value and worth doing will have a significant cost, but our God will and can supply all our needs through his grace and power in Christ (Philippians 4:19).

The Reward

This entire book in many ways is a tribute to the rewards we have gained by adopting Jacob and the reward you can gain by practicing true religion in your life. In addition to the spiritual lessons Jeanie has written about, I also think of the simple satisfaction of knowing we practiced James 1:27 in our house, our family and our church. There is the joy of knowing that because we have adopted, others have been encouraged to do so. It is my prayer that because of this book Jacob will figuratively become the father of many abandoned children who find families, as Jeanie has already alluded to. There is no way we could have seen our family and individual parts of it mature in ways we have without the choice to adopt Jacob.

And finally, I believe in my heart of hearts that there will be a special "Well done, good and faithful servant!" from the Father and the Son as more and more disciples defend the cause of the fatherless and practice true religion.

I thank God for taking me on Jacob's Journey!

Jacob walking Mom down the aisle at Melissa's wedding

About the Author

Jeanie Whitehead Shaw grew up in Gainesville, Florida, where she became a Christian as a teenager. She graduated from the University of Florida, where she met her husband-to-be, Wyndham Shaw. As a young married couple, they worked for five years in the campus ministry in Raleigh, North Carolina, serving the campuses of North Carolina State, the University of North Carolina and Duke University. Then, over an eight-year period, they worked with the churches in Morgantown, West Virginia, and Charlotte, North Carolina.

For the past fourteen years they have been with the church in Boston, where they currently serve as elder and wife, and evangelist and women's ministry leader. Wyndham now also serves as the Executive Director of HOPE *worldwide* New England, a non-profit benevolent organization. Jeanie serves as Director of Program Development. She develops programs such as the HOPE *worldwide* Family Center in Romania and the New England Permanent Families Program, which includes foster care, home studies, post-placement training and support, and various other programs throughout the Northeast and Europe. Through HOPE *worldwide*, she is also a representative to the United Nations advisory council.

Jeanie and Wyndham have four children: Melissa, Kristen, Sam and Jacob, and they have one son "by marriage": Kevin Miller, who is married to Melissa. They are raising an exemplary family, and have taught innumerable classes and seminars on marriage and family. They are known in the churches worldwide for their wisdom, compassion and insight.

Jacob with Maria ("Grandmother" and "Angel") in Romania

Jeanie, Jacob and Wyndham after the adoption ceremony in the States

CHAPTER APPLICATION QUESTIONS
AND ADDITIONAL SCRIPTURES

Chapter 1 - The Big Picture
- In what areas of your life do you find it most difficult to trust God?
- What does it mean to you that it is God's heart to adopt you, give you his love and make you his heir?
- What day-to-day activities are blocking your view of the "big picture"?
- What are some ways that God has shown you that he wants to enjoy being your Father?

For further study:
Isaiah 55:8-9
Romans 8:15-17
1 Corinthians 2:9

Chapter 2 - God Is Searching
- Are you afraid to dream? Why or why not?
- What dreams have you abandoned?
- Where were you when God reached out to you?
- What are the fears that keep you from pursuing God's dreams for your life?

For further study:
1 Chronicles 28:9
Psalm 138:8
Isaiah 26:12
Acts 17:24-28

Chapter 3 – Jacob's Shoes
- What does Jesus see in your heart and your life as he walks in your shoes? How does he help you?
- Think of the people God has put in your life. Whose "shoes" do you need to walk in so that you can better understand them?

For further study:
Mark 2:8
1 Corinthians 9:19-22
1 Peter 3:8

Chapter 4 – It Doesn't Make Sense
- Joseph's conviction to trust God above himself was enough. Is yours?
- What are some circumstances in your life right now that are tempting you to not trust God? By faith, how can God bring good in these situations?
- Who are some men and women in the Bible who, like Joseph, trusted God when the odds weren't looking so good? Who are some men and women in your local church who have also trusted God in tough times? How can you imitate these men and women of faith?

For further study:
2 Corinthians 4:7-10
Hebrews 6:10
Hebrews 11:1-2

Chapter 5 – What's in a Name?

- If you are a disciple of Jesus, are you secure in God's grace?
- How does it make you feel to know that God gave you his Spirit as a guarantee of your inheritance?
- How can this identity in God's family change the way you live this week?

For further study:
Isaiah 62:2
John 10:28-29
2 Corinthians 5:5
Revelation 2:17

Chapter 6 – Counting the Cost

- When have you been tempted to run away from God?
- What are some lies that Satan is trying to fill your mind with to entice you to give in to fear and doubt?
- In what ways do you need to step out into the unknown? Do it! Have a strong, spiritual friend help you along the way.

For further study:
Romans 15:13
Hebrews 11:6
Hebrews 11:13-16
James 4:7

Chapter 7 – God Will Provide

- In which situations do you need reminding that God is working in your life?
- Who are some *Marias* that God has put in your life to help, comfort or guide you?
- What are some ways that God has miraculously provided in your life (or in the life of someone you know)? How does this affect your faith?

For further study:
Nehemiah 9:19-21
Philippians 4:14-19
2 Peter 1:3

Chapter 8 – Leaving the Past Behind

- What "old clothes" do you hold on to that should be thrown in the corner?
- Write in your own words how God views you in your "new clothes"—given to you when you were baptized into Christ.
- Do you view other Christians in their "old clothes" or in their "new clothes"? How would God want you to view them?

For further study:
2 Corinthians 5:16-17
Colossians 3:9-14
Revelation 3:18

Chapter 9 – Anticipating the Journey

- When was a time you thought a journey had ended but realized that a new journey had just begun?
- In what area of your life do you need to infuse new energy and anticipation?
- What can you do today to revitalize your relationship with God with the excitement and wonder you had when you were first studying the Bible?

For further study:
Joshua 14:10-12
Psalm 84:5-7
Revelation 2:4-5

Chapter 10 – A Rich Welcome

- What do you imagine heaven to be?
- Besides God and Jesus, who will be one of the first people you will want to talk to in heaven? What questions will you ask?
- Who do you need to help get to heaven? How are you helping them?

For further study:
Luke 15:3-7
Hebrews 12:22-24
Revelation 21

Chapter 11 – 'Leessss Go!'

- Do you have a "Leessss go!" attitude toward life?
- In what areas are you hesitant and passive? How can you put "one foot after the other" to become more active in conquering complacency?
- Who are some people in your life who have become critical or fearful? How can you help them to become active and excited?

For further study:
Numbers 14:24
1 Samuel 14:1-14
Romans 12:11

Chapter 12 – 'I'm Good at Punch!'

- What do you most want to excel in?
- If you have children, what do you most want them to excel in?
- What fruit of the Spirit can you develop, exercise and become strong in?

For further study:
Galatians 5:22-23
Colossians 3:23-24
1 John 3:21-22

Chapter 13 – 'I Don't Know That Word'
- Is there an area in your life in which you have not had a teachable heart? If so, how will you change?
- Answer honestly: When you find yourself being prideful or stubborn with someone, do you ever stop and pray aloud with that person? When you do, how does it affect your heart?
- What have you been learning in God's word lately? How have you been applying it to your life?

For further study:
Proverbs 13:10
Proverbs 18:12
James 3:13

Chapter 14 – The Victory Is in the Hard Stuff
- What are some times in your walk with God that he soaked you in his unconditional love when you felt you least deserved it?
- Who is someone to whom you can show that same kind of unconditional love this week?
- Is there anything in your life that you are grieving over? Are you being open with others who can help you through this process? Most importantly, are you being open with God?

For further study:
2 Samuel 22:36
1 Corinthians 15:57
James 5:11

Chapter 15 – Somewhere Out There

- How does it make you feel to know that God "rejoices over you with singing"? What love song can you imagine him singing to you?
- What can you do to make God's presence more real to you?
- Do you have a love song to sing to God in response to his love?

For further study:
Exodus 15:1-21
Judges 5:1-3
Psalm 89:1-2

Chapter 16 – 'Be Careful My Passport'

- Compare your life before God and your life now. Do you sometimes miss the "old" life? What are the things you miss?
- What are the blessings of your "new" life in God?
- Have you prayed to God, thanking him for how much he has spared you?

For further study:
Deuteronomy 8:2-4
Nehemiah 9:17
Psalm 73:21-26

Chapter 17 – 'It Takes Time, Dad'
- How is your patience lately?
- How has God demonstrated his perfect patience in your life?
- Who do you need to exercise patience with by seeing their progress instead of their faults?

For further study:
Isaiah 29:16
Isaiah 64:8
1 Corinthians 13:4
Hebrews 12:2-11

Chapter 18 – Stones of Remembrance
- What stones of remembrance are you creating in your life?
- What stones of remembrance are you helping others to create?
- What important events are coming up that will give you an opportunity to create some special memories—either for yourself or for someone else?

For further study:
Genesis 9:12-17
Exodus 20:11
Luke 22:19

Chapter 19 – Melissa's Story
- Do you spend time thinking about specific ways to encourage those you are close to? How can you make this kind of encouragement a priority in your life?
- Who are some people on the "outskirts" that you can pull into your life? How will you do this?
- Do you tend to generate unity or division in your relationships? How can you be more loving and unified with those around you?

For further study:
John 17:20-23
1 Corinthians 11:1-13:13
Hebrews 10:25

Chapter 20 – Love Spreads
- What words of praise do you spread about God to others?
- Are you eager or reluctant to praise people to their faces? Do you fear that people will not be as impressed with you if you are intent on praising others? If so, how can you change this?
- Who is someone that you can specifically encourage and build up this week?

For further study:
Proverbs 15:23
Luke 4:22
1 Thessalonians 5:11

Chapter 21 – Kristen's Perspective
- What are some of the challenges that you have faced (or are currently facing)? Do you ask God for help? Do you ask others for help?
- Is there any bitterness or anger in your heart because of things that have happened in your life? Have you wrestled with God about these things?
- Considering any challenges you have faced along life's journey, what are some things you've learned that you can help others with?

For further study:
Psalm 6:2
Isaiah 57:18-19
Jeremiah 29:11-13
2 Corinthians 12:7-10

Chapter 22 – 'Sam No Pajamas, Me No Pajamas'
- Who are the men or women in your life that you look up to and want to imitate?
- What qualities do these people have that draw you to them? Have you recently shared with them your respect and gratitude for them?
- Are you an example of Christ to others? What can you change to be a better example?

For further study:
1 Corinthians 4:15-16
Philippians 3:17
1 Thessalonians 2:8

Chapter 23 – Sam Speaks

- In your relationships, do you tend to retaliate or to withdraw when you are hurt? How does either response affect others? How does God want you to respond when you are hurt?
- In what ways do you pull away from God when you are hurt or disappointed?
- What can you do this week to build a stronger unconditional love in your relationship with God? With others?

For further study:
Deuteronomy 7:7-9
2 Kings 4:11-37
Psalm 32

Chapter 24 – Iron Man

- What does it mean in your life that when you are weak, you are strong?
- Do you put a protective shell around your heart? If so, why are you afraid to be open and vulnerable with others?
- What can you do this week to express vulnerability and emotions to God? To others?

For further study:
Psalm 88
Matthew 9:20-22
Matthew 26:37-39

Chapter 25 – 'Don't Forget Me'

- What are some of your favorite promises (assurances) from God's word?
- What are some specific things you can do to reassure people in your life that they are special?
- In what ways do others cause you to feel special? Have you ever told them how much these things mean to you?

For further study:
Deuteronomy 31:8
Isaiah 49:15-16
Matthew 28:18-20

Chapter 26 – Things Aren't Always As They Seem

- How are your listening skills? What can you do to sharpen them?
- Is there a situation lately in which you "assumed" something and came to the wrong conclusion? How can you correct the situation?
- How can you train yourself to ask questions for clarification rather than jump to erroneous conclusions?

For further study:
Joshua 22
Proverbs 1:5
Matthew 7:1-5

Chapter 27 – 'Who's the Big Guy Here?'

- Who is the "big guy" in your life? How does this affect your decisions?
- What "giants" are stopping you from stepping out on faith with God?
- Who else do you sometimes try to please when you forget that God is the big guy? How does this affect you spiritually?

For further study:
1 Samuel 17
Job 37:14-24
Hebrews 10:35-39

Chapter 28 – Who Am I?

- Do you view the Bible as a rulebook or as a love letter from God?
- Write down some ways that God showed his love to us through Jesus.
- Do you view people with a spiritual identity, or do you see people according to their culture, background, intelligence or race? How does God view you?

For further study:
2 Corinthians 5:14-16
Colossians 1:25-27
Hebrews 1:1-3

Chapter 29 – Keepin' It Simple
- Does God feel loved by you? If not, what can you do to express that love?
- Would you say you ever send a "form letter" back to God after reading his "love letter" to you?
- Is there an area in your life where the "walk" doesn't match the "talk"? What can you study in your Bible to help change this? Do you know someone who has strength in this area who can help you? Seek that help!

For further study:
John 21:15-19
Ephesians 5:10
1 John 2:6

Chapter 30 – 'My Decision'
- Write in your own words what it means to you to have freedom of choice.
- How does your freedom of choice affect your relationship with God?
- How does it make you feel to know that God has chosen to love you?

For further study:
Deuteronomy 30:11-20
Isaiah 53
Mark 10:17-27
Luke 15:11-32
1 John 4:19

Chapter 31 – The Advocate
- In what ways has Jesus been your advocate? What does this mean to you?
- Who can you be an advocate for?
- Why does it require unselfishness to be someone's advocate?

For further study:
Isaiah 53:12
Romans 8:31-39
Hebrews 7:25

Chapter 32 – The Road Race
- How is your "race" going? Are you eagerly running, slowing down or barely crawling?
- Describe (from imagination or experience) what it feels like to cross the finish line in a race. Now describe what you think it is going to feel like to cross the finish line in heaven. What "spiritual muscles" do you need to strengthen to make it?
- How well do you encourage and help other people to cross their finish lines?

For further study:
1 Corinthians 9:24-27
Philippians 3:12-14
Revelation 21:7

Chapter 33 – 'I Used to Be That Kid'

- What situations have you hardened yourself to in order to protect yourself emotionally? What is the outcome spiritually when you do this?
- What situation have you been in when you didn't want to stop giving? How God must have smiled when he saw that!
- Are there times when you become annoyed with the people around you? Why do you think that is? How should you respond when this is happening?

For further study:
Matthew 7:12
John 3:16-17
Colossians 3:13-14

Chapter 34 – Ready and Waiting

- Did you see yourself in Jacob's stubbornness? What situations tempt you to be stubborn? How do you typically respond to this temptation?
- How do you do when a conflict is not resolved? Are you willing to stay with the person until you are reconnected?
- Why do you think it is so very difficult to be humble when we are wrong or when we have hurt someone?

For further study:
Isaiah 50:5
Jeremiah 7:22-24
Matthew 5:23-24
Ephesians 4:1-6

Chapter 35 – The Judge
- Describe how you view God as the Judge. How does this affect your relationship with him?
- Considering the mercy God has shown to you, how merciful have you been to others?

For further study:
Isaiah 1:18
Psalm 96:13
Hebrews 12:22-24
1 Peter 1:3

Chapter 36 – Citizenship
- Do you think often about heaven? What do you think it will be like?
- What are the freedoms and privileges of being a disciple of Jesus?
- Who are the "top ten" people you want to take to heaven with you? How are you helping them on their journey?

For further study:
John 14:1-3
1 Peter 1:3-9
2 Peter 3:13
Revelation 21

Jacob with his karate trophies

Jacob in his soccer uniform

Who Are We?

Discipleship Publications International (DPI) began publishing in 1993. We are a nonprofit Christian publisher affiliated with the International Churches of Christ, committed to publishing and distributing materials that honor God, lift up Jesus Christ and show how his message practically applies to all areas of life. We have a deep conviction that no one changes life like Jesus and that the implementation of his teaching will revolutionize any life, any marriage, any family and any singles household.

Since our beginning we have published more than 100 titles; plus we have produced a number of important, spiritual audio products. More than one million volumes have been printed, and our works have been translated into more than a dozen languages—international is not just a part of our name! Our books are shipped regularly to every inhabited continent.

To see a more detailed description of our works, find us on the World Wide Web at www.dpibooks.org. You can order books by calling 1-888-DPI-BOOK 24 hours a day. From outside the US, call 978-670-8840 during Boston-area business hours.

We appreciate the hundreds of comments we have received from readers. We would love to hear from you. Here are other ways to get in touch:

Mail: DPI, 2 Sterling Road, Billerica, Mass. 01862-2595
E-mail: dpibooks@icoc.org

Find Us on the
World Wide Web

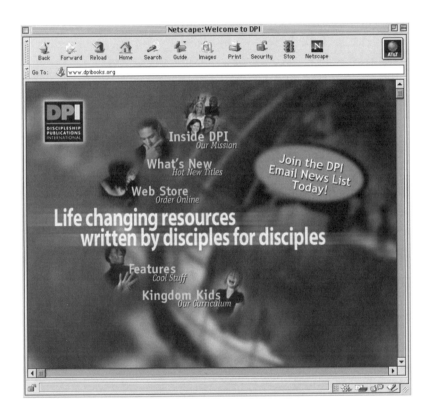

www.dpibooks.org